CHARLES WESLEY

The Wesley Historical Society Lecture No. 14
Bristol Conference
A Synopsis of which was delivered at the New Room,
Broadmead, Bristol
16th July 1948

Charles Wesley, from the portrait by
John Russell, B.A.

CHARLES WESLEY

As Revealed by His Letters

BY

FRANK BAKER
B.A., B.D.

WIPF & STOCK · Eugene, Oregon

Wipf and Stock Publishers
199 W 8th Ave, Suite 3
Eugene, OR 97401

Charles Wesley
As Revealed by His Letters
By Baker, Frank
Copyright©1948 Methodist Publishing - Epworth Press
ISBN 13: 978-1-5326-3068-2
Publication date 4/6/2017
Previously published by Epworth Press, 1948

Every effort has been made to trace the current copyright
owner of this publication but without success. If you have
any information or interest in the copyright, please contact the publishers.

CONTENTS

	FOREWORD	iv
	BIOGRAPHICAL SUMMARY. . .	v
	INTRODUCTION	1
1.	OXFORD DAYS	7
2.	AMERICAN INTERLUDE . . .	20
3.	METHODIST PREACHER . . .	32
4.	DUBLIN'S FAIR CITY . . .	44
5.	SALLY GWYNNE	54
6.	FOR BETTER FOR WORSE . .	68
7.	PURGING THE PREACHERS . .	79
8.	THE OLD SHIP	91
9.	PATERFAMILIAS	104
10.	CURE OF SOULS	117
11.	ORDINATION IS SEPARATION . .	129
12.	SWEET SINGER	141
	INDEX	151

ILLUSTRATIONS

CHARLES WESLEY. *From the portrait by John Russell, R.A.* . . . *Frontis.*

LETTER FROM CHARLES WESLEY TO SALLY GWYNNE, WRITTEN DURING THEIR COURTSHIP *facing p.* 10

FOREWORD

My hearty thanks are due to the following libraries and individuals, who have allowed transcriptions of manuscript letters by Charles Wesley to be made, and extracts to be published: Bodleian Library, Oxford; British Province of the Church of the United Brethren, London; Emory University Library, Georgia, U.S.A. (photostats, and transcriptions by Mr. R. B. Harwell); Methodist Historical Society of New York (transcription by Dr. J. R. Joy); Methodist Mission House, London; National Library of Wales, Aberystwyth (transcriptions by the Revs. C. Deane Little and Griffith T. Roberts, M.A., B.D.); New Room, Bristol (collation by the Rev. E. T. Selby); Public Records Office, London; Richmond College, Surrey (old transcriptions made by Thomas Marriott); Rylands Library, Manchester; Wesley's House, London; Maggs Bros., Ltd., London; Myers & Co. Ltd., London; the Rev. F. F. Bretherton, B.A., Sunderland; Dr. Elmer T. Clark, New York; the Rev. R. Lee Cole, M.A., B.D., Dublin; Mrs. E. Lawson, Plymouth; Bishop F. D. Leete, St. Petersburg, Florida, U.S.A.; Mr. Sydney Raine, Birmingham. More detailed acknowledgements can be made when it is eventually possible to publish the collected edition of Charles Wesley's letters on which I am working. I must single out for special thanks the Rev. Edgar C. Barton and the Rev. Frank H. Cumbers, B.A., B.D., and members of the staff at the Methodist Book Room, London, for so readily making available their unique collection of Wesley manuscripts.

I am greatly indebted to the President of the Wesley Historical Society, the Rev. F. F. Bretherton, B.A., and to the Rev. Wesley F. Swift, Assistant Editor of the Society's *Proceedings*, who have both proved true friends by reading the typescript and by making valuable suggestions and criticisms.

FRANK BAKER

WARSOP
January 1948

PREFACE TO REVISED EDITION

On pp. 128–29 of the second edition of *Charles Wesley's Verse: An Introduction* I belatedly took the opportunity of pointing out my serious historical *faux pas* in the first edition of this present volume (p. 25). My source was John Telford's *The Life of the Rev. Charles Wesley, M.A.*, revised and enlarged edition, London, Wesleyan Methodist Book Room, 1900. On pp. 245–46 Telford described at some length how in 'records and correspondence of the early colonists', then in the custody of the Georgia Historical Society, a named magazine writer had discovered a 1736 letter by Charles Wesley, written from Jekyl Island, Georgia, to the wife of General James Oglethorpe. It described the origin of a hymn later used by Wesley to describe Land's End in Cornwall, beginning: 'Lo! on a narrow neck of land,/ 'Twixt two unbounded seas, I stand—', 'which, I trust, may pleasure your ladyship'. Naturally I wrote from England to Savannah for some verification of the letter, but receiving no replies to my suspicious letters of inquiry, I felt compelled during the haste of publication to rely on Telford's authority. In fact, however, this was a literary hoax, which neither Telford nor I had suspected, not having checked that Oglethorpe was not married until 1743. (In later years I have found the Georgia Historical Society very helpful indeed, but the unwitting harm had already been caused!) The forgery had been prepared for reading before the Chicago Literary Club in December 1892 by Franklin Harvey Head (1832–1914), and privately printed 'for the amusement of his friends' in a four-page pamphlet, *Studies in Early American History, The Legends of Jekyl Island*. A salutary warning never to trust a secondary source!

Frank Baker

Duke University
September 5, 1995

The Proceeds from This Revised Volume Are to Be Used by The Charles Wesley Society

BIOGRAPHICAL SUMMARY

1703	June 28	John Wesley born.
1707	Dec. 18	Charles Wesley born.
1716	April	Entered Westminster School.
1726	June 13	Matriculated at Christ Church College, Oxford.
	Oct. 12	Sarah Gwynne born.
1729	January	Began to keep a diary.
	(March?)	Formed nucleus of the Holy Club.
	November	John Wesley returned to Oxford, becoming leader of Holy Club.
1730		Graduated B.A., became tutor at Oxford.
1732		Introduced George Whitefield to the Holy Club.
1733	March 12	Graduated M.A.
1735	April 25	Rev. Samuel Wesley, rector of Epworth, died.
	Sept. 21	Ordained deacon by Dr. John Potter, Bishop of Oxford.
	Sept. 24	Appointed Secretary for Indian Affairs, Georgia.
	Sept. 29	Ordained priest by Dr. Edmund Gibson, Bishop of London.
	Oct. 14	Embarked for Georgia.
1736	March 9	Took up ministry in Frederica. Commenced published journal.
	July 26	Left Georgia for England.
	Dec. 3	Landed in England.
1738	April 3	Resigned his Georgia secretaryship.
	May 21	Experienced 'conversion'.
	Oct. 20	First preached without notes.

1739	May 29	First preached in fields.
	Nov. 6	Rev. Samuel Wesley, Master of Tiverton, died.
1742	July 23	Mrs. Susanna Wesley died.
1747	Sept. 9– March 20, 1748	First visit to Ireland.
1748	Aug. 13– Oct. 8	Second visit to Ireland.
1749		Published *Hymns and Sacred Poems*.
	April 8	Married Sarah Gwynne.
	Sept. 1	Set up house in Charles Street, Bristol.
	Oct. 2	John Bennet and Grace Murray married.
1751	Feb. 18?	John Wesley and Mrs. Vazeille married.
1752	August	Son John Wesley born.
1756	Sept.–Oct.	Last northern journey.
1757	Dec. 11	Son Charles born.
1759	April 1	Daughter Sarah born.
1762		Published *Short Hymns on Select Passages of the Holy Scriptures*.
1766	Feb. 24	Son Samuel born.
1771		Family removed to Chesterfield Street, Marylebone.
1784	Sept. 1–2	John Wesley ordained preachers for America.
1788	March 29	Charles Wesley died.
	April 5	Charles Wesley buried in Marylebone churchyard.
1822	Dec. 22	Mrs. Charles Wesley died.

INTRODUCTION

CHARLES WESLEY is not as well known, even amongst Methodists, as he deserves to be. This seems at first very surprising, in view of the generally acknowledged fact that his hymns were such a strong formative influence in the Methodist Revival, and have since become the treasured possession of the Church Universal. The main reason for the comparative neglect of Charles Wesley is, of course, John Wesley. John has completely overshadowed his younger brother. Reasons are not far to seek. John Wesley's was the more dominant personality. His gift of leadership was far greater. Their views on the relationship between the Methodist societies and the Church of England differed considerably, John being led almost without knowing it—certainly without acknowledging it—into a separation, from which Charles was continually striving to pull him back, occasionally with a severe scolding thrown in. Similarly Charles Wesley did not favour the enhanced status which was accorded by his brother to their lay helpers. Because of these differences Charles kept the peace by retiring into semi-obscurity, a course to which he was urged by the breakdown in his health, and also in a lesser degree by family responsibilities. So it was that Methodism came to be identified both with the views and with the person of John Wesley, whilst 'brother Charles' remained for most people very much in the background.

In spite of this, however, more worthy appreciation would probably have been his had his life been easier to document. For John Wesley's many biographers there has been an abundance of material—in particular his incomparable *Journal*, and nearly three thousand letters, loyally preserved by his hero-worshipping followers. With Charles the situation is quite different. Though he kept a journal from 1729, he published no extracts from it. When eventually most of what still remained was presented to the world, in 1849, it was found to be very uneven, covering the years 1736–51 with occasional fullness but with serious gaps, and supplemented by valuable remnants for December 1753, July–August 1754, and September–November 1756. Two other important sources remained for the would-be biographer—his hymns and his letters. The hymns were known to be in many cases reflections of the poet's personal life, yet their biographical value was very limited because only in a few cases could they be accurately dated. Turning to the letters, once again disappointment was in store.

Charles Wesley's letters do not appear to have been preserved with anything like the devotion accorded to those of his brother. The unfamiliar handwriting, and the lack of a signature, have probably caused hundreds to be discarded as of little value. There has never been any real attempt to publish them. To the two volumes of his *Journal* published by the Rev. Thomas Jackson in 1849, however, were appended 'selections from his correspondence and poetry'. Jackson's selection comprises 106 letters. The perusal of this collection soon reveals another significant obstacle against the full use of the letters as biographical material. Like the hymns, though less excusably, they are for the most part insufficiently dated. Of the 106, only 40 are fully dated, and one of those wrongly, from a faulty reading by the editor of an endorsement by the recipient, Mrs. Wesley. Jackson's noble attempt to place them in chronological order has in a few places broken down badly.[1]

Official correspondence, of which little appears to have

---

[1] e.g. Letters 71–92, which were presumably in the correct chronological order. The following are the actual years of their writing, all of which had to be deduced except Nos. 71, 73, 88, 91, and 92: 1766: 1760?: 1768: 1763: 1759: 1759: 1759: 1766: 1760: 1759: 1766: 1759: 1770?: 1766: 1766: 1763: 1771: 1771: 1764?: 1784: 1777: 1778.

survived, Charles Wesley seems usually to have both signed and dated. Amongst his friends, however, he was remiss in both particulars—having no idea, of course, that posterity might be interested in the matter. Almost half of his extant letters were written to his wife. Of about 250 so far transcribed (all but five from the original manuscripts), there is not one signed, and only five initialled, whilst only 36 are adequately dated. The record is better for other correspondents, however, especially in his later years. About half the extant letters to his children are fully dated and either signed or initialled, and a slightly smaller proportion of his correspondence outside the family. Three only of the letters so far seen bear the simple signature 'Charles': those written in the 1770's to his old friend James Hutton. Usually his letters ended with an abrupt 'Farewell' or 'Adieu', and he could even write 'Yours affectionately' without appending any signature.

The letters to his wife are in many ways the most interesting and valuable. Usually they begin, however, something like this—'The F[oundery], July 24', or even 'Litchfield Street, Sunday'. The year, and even the month, obvious enough to the recipient, have to be painfully deduced by the biographer. This is all the more annoying when we compare the meticulous secretarial care of John Wesley, who hardly ever omitted such details. Thus the biographer of Charles Wesley must be very cautious when quoting from his letters. Indeed he cannot safely use them to any extent until the literary detective has been at work, patiently establishing their correct dates, sometimes from very slight clues. Fortunately Methodism is rich in biographies and letters which help in the elucidation of these clues, though some lines of investigation can only be followed up in such avenues as contemporary periodicals, road maps, calendars, and even tables of the moon's phases. Gradually, however, some order emerges from the chaos. Many letters can be dated with certainty, sometimes confirming dates previously suggested by Jackson or the Rev. John Telford, but occasionally proving them to have been mistaken. A number of the manuscripts have been endorsed by Mrs. Charles Wesley or others, though not all of these endorsements prove to be reliable. Some of the letters may be assigned to related groups, and the combination of clues helps to date the group as a whole. The fact that Charles Wesley was the father of a family proves of great assistance, so that letters may be dated from the mention of such details as young Sally's 'meazles', or Sammy's 'invisible tormentors'—his first teeth. Occasionally, however, it seems that a letter might belong to any one of twenty or thirty years, and only by a wearisome process of elimination can the field be narrowed, and the actual year be found, or approximately found.

All this literary spadework is abundantly worth while, however. In preparation for a collected edition of Charles Wesley's letters the author has made transcripts of about 600, all but about 100 from the original manuscripts.[1] Some 250 of these have already been published, though in many cases either as extracts only, or with omissions small or large. Of the 600 letters transcribed—speaking roughly—230 were adequately dated by Charles Wesley himself. The dates of 265 more have been deduced with certainty, and of 75 with some probability. Only a small remnant of eight so far remains without even approximate dates assigned.

Another difficulty about Charles Wesley's letters is that a good number are available only in shorthand copies, made either on the back of the letter being answered or on some other handy piece of paper. In writing to his

---

[1] Actually not all are 'originals'; some are drafts or copies made by Charles Wesley himself, varying slightly from the letters themselves.

brother John he often introduced shorthand into the actual letters themselves, in addition to Latin and Greek! This was not to save space, of course, but for the sake of secrecy—a tantalizing challenge to the inquisitive student! We must therefore turn to a study of John Byrom's *Universal English Short-Hand*. Again many snags appear. For Byrom's shorthand, like Pitman's (which closely resembles it in a few particulars), gives for most words only an outline of the consonants, whilst a good deal of contraction is possible. Even when imagination is given a free rein it sometimes reaches no satisfactory goal. Nor was Charles Wesley always such a copperplate penman as has sometimes been assumed. Although the letters written to his brother in shorthand are usually very neat, this is not so when we come to the copies made for his own use. Passages which present a superficial appearance of neatness may have been so hurriedly written that the characters are wrongly sloped or badly finished, even to the extent of actually meaning something quite different from what was intended. Yet we must be grateful for these scraps of shorthand, with their difficulties and uncertainties, for in many cases they have rescued letters which would otherwise have been lost.

A satisfactory full-length biography of Charles Wesley cannot yet be written, though it is well worth the writing, for much preliminary spadework has still to be done on his letters, many of which must even yet be lying unpublished and practically unknown in the hands of libraries and private owners.[1] On the basis of the work already done in collecting and dating the letters, however, we offer this brief sketch of the poet of Methodism as revealed by his letters alone. As far as possible Charles Wesley has been allowed to speak for himself, by quotations from over two hundred representative letters, more than half of which are here published for the first time.

[1] The author would be glad to hear of any such, c/o The Epworth Press.

Perhaps a word should be added about the literary worth of the letters. Here we cannot but agree with John Wesley's tribute—'I am very sensible that writing letters is my brother's talent rather than mine'. This is certainly high praise, for John Wesley's own letters are among the clearest, the most terse and direct in the world. Yet their very strength is also their weakness, for they usually lack colour and warmth. Whilst Charles Wesley can be just as concise as his brother, and even more aphoristic, his letters are usually more rounded off; there are more touches of humour and of tenderness, more passages of description and exhortation, more variety. Charles was primarily a poet, not a logician, and his letters undoubtedly reveal a greater sense of the rhythm and melody of words than do those of his brother. They are a worthy contribution to literature, as well as to biography and history, although that is not here our main concern.

NOTE: For the comfort of the reader, Charles Wesley's spelling and punctuation have been modernized, and the many abbreviations extended. His lavish use of capitals also has been pruned in conformity with modern taste. Because of the uncertainty of some of the transcriptions from his shorthand, it has been felt advisable to distinguish them by using italics, which are also used for his frequent underlinings. It may be assumed, in the absence of a note to the contrary, that a *sentence* in italics represents a transcription from the shorthand, while a *word* or *phrase* so distinguished denotes Charles Wesley's underlining. In all cases brackets [ ] denote explanatory additions or substitutions, and parentheses with a note of interrogation (?) passages where the manuscript is defective or indecipherable.

CHAPTER I

OXFORD DAYS

THE average schoolboy is not much addicted to writing letters home. And as young Charles Wesley seems to have been a fair sample of the average schoolboy, his brief communications with the family at Epworth rectory would probably consist mainly of requests for pocket-money. It is not surprising that none of them seem to have survived. The main facts of his early education were outlined in a biographical letter of 28th April 1785:

> At eight years old, in 1716, I was sent by my father, rector of Epworth, to Westminster School, and placed under the care of my eldest brother Samuel, a strict Churchman, who brought me up in his own principles. My brother John, five years older than me, was then at the Charterhouse. In 1727 I was elected Student of Christ Church. My brother John was then Fellow of Lincoln.

A reminiscence of the stern discipline of those early days is found in a letter of 1749, advising Mrs. Jones of Fonmon about her headstrong son:

> If Robin *will* not be led, he must be driven. I mean whipped through Westminster or some other great school.

Not that Charles himself was actually 'whipped through Westminster'. After all, he was under the protection of a rather indulgent elder brother, who occupied the proud position of usher or undermaster of the school where he himself had been educated. Although nearly seventeen years his senior, the Rev. Samuel Wesley, M.A., had a real affection for his youngest brother. Not only did he combine with John to meet the expenses of Charles' education, but also helped to fashion his churchmanship and his love of the classics of Greece and Rome. Until Samuel died prematurely in 1739 there existed between them a very close bond of sympathy, though Charles found Samuel's short-tempered wife Nutty rather a trial—for he himself suffered from an unstable temperament. Yet when he had been elected to Christ Church College, Oxford, after having attained the proud position of Captain of Westminster School, he still came back to his brother's home in Dean's Yard for vacations.

It was after one such holiday that he wrote his first extant letter, on his mother's birthday, 20th January 1728, addressed 'To the Revd. Mr. John Wesley, Curate at Epworth in the Isle of Axholm near Wroot'. Carefree Oxford was a relief after the tense atmosphere at Westminster:

I breathe once again, a free though sharp air. . . . You needn't fear my giving in to my sister's persuasion, who would willingly have me think you don't care a farthing for me, and is desirous I should care just as much for you. But this trial of my passive valour is at last over. . . . She is at London, and I at Oxford!

Genuine family affection is seen in his brief account of tragically-mated Hetty Wesley, ten years his senior:

One sister I parted from with great regret. . . . Poor Sister Hetty! It grieves me almost to think how exceedingly kindly she treated me, who am seldom so happy as to meet with bare humanity from others. 'Tis a shocking comparison! 'Twas but a week before I left London that I knew she was at it. Little of that time, you may be sure, did I lose, being with her almost continually. I could almost envy myself the deal of pleasure I had crowded within that small space. In a little neat room she has hired did the goodnatured, ingenious, contented wretch and I talk over a few short days which we both wished had been longer. As yet she lives pretty well, having but herself and honest Will [Wright] to keep, though I fancy there's another acoming. Brother and sister are very kind to her, and I (hope?) will continue so: for I have cautioned her never to contradict my sister, whom she knows.

This first letter struck a note that was often sounded during Charles Wesley's Oxford days—his financial needs. Yet he managed to be jaunty even in his poverty, telling how he and his friend Bob Kirkham had reacted to 'that plaguy piece of news' that John Wesley could not be expected to return to Oxford, being 'settled for life—at least for years':

'Twill most certainly have one of two widely-different effects upon me: make me a very hard student, or none at all; an excellent economist, or a poor desperate scoundrel; a Patient Grizzle like Moll, or a Grumbletonial like Pat.[1] 'Tis in the power of a few Epworth or Wroot guineas and clothes to give things the favourable turn, and make a gentleman of me. Come Money then, and quickly, to rescue me from my melancholy maxim, ex nihilo nihil fit—I can possibly save nothing, where there's nothing to be saved.

The prospect of John's continued absence moved Charles to his earliest known verse:

Nor yet from my dim eyes THY form retires!

(The cold empty starving grate before me makes me add the following disconsolate line:)

Nor cheering image of thine absent fires.

He went on to portray in unfinished lines the pleasant hours spent with Bob Kirkham's sisters, and their friends Mary Pendarves and Anne Granville:

Hinxy's
No longer now on Horrel's airy van,
With thee shall I admire the subject plain,
Or where the sight in neighbouring shades is lost,
Or where the lengthened prospect widens most;
While or ye tuneful poet's (something) song,
Or truths divine flow easy from thy tongue.

---

[1] Charles referred to his sisters Mary and Martha. 'Grumbletonian' was a nickname given to supporters of the Country as opposed to the Court Party.

'Horrel's airy van' was a favourite rendezvous of the little coterie, a beech-clad hill-crest overlooking Stanton, where in lovely surroundings the wit of Mrs. Pendarves and the solid learning and shrewd reasoning of John Wesley were outmatched by the devout sweetness of their 'dear Varanese', Mrs. Chapone, formerly Sally Kirkham. Later in the letter the Kirkham home was again mentioned:

> Bob heard a few days ago from Stanton, where they're all well, as he shall tell you more particularly if I can light on him by and by. What say you to a visit next summer? Won't that tempt you up? *You* don't insist upon an invitation. If this won't fetch you nothing will.

John Wesley did revisit Oxford (and presumably Stanton) that summer, when he was ordained priest by Bishop Potter. Soon, however, he resumed his duties in Lincolnshire as his father's curate. In later years he thus described Charles's outlook at this period:

> He pursued his studies diligently, and led a regular, harmless life; but if I spoke to him about religion he would warmly answer, 'What! would you have me be a saint all at once?' and would hear no more.

During John's visit, however, something happened to Charles. The prospect of being a saint seemed more attractive, though little nearer. His spiritual pilgrimage had begun, though not for another ten years did he come within sight of the Promised Land. On 22nd January 1729 he wrote to John:

> God has thought fit (it may be to increase my wariness) to deny me at present your company and assistance. 'Tis through Him strengthening me I trust to maintain my ground till we meet, and neither before or after that time shall I, I hope, relapse into my former state of insensibility. 'Tis through your means, I firmly believe, God will establish what He has begun in me, and there is no one person I would so willingly have to be the instrument of good to me as you.
>
> I verily think, dear brother, I shall never quarrel with *you*

March 2nd Bristol
1749

Be of good comfort. Jesus loves you, & shall make all things work together for yr good. Cast yr care upon Him. Fear not. All Power is given unto Him, wch He employs in our Salvation. Be confident He cannot chuse amiss. You shall be Happy (with or without Instruments) in Him alone. —— I expected Tri-als, before we are suffered to meet. The Lord bear all yr Brethren, & lead yu thro' things Temporal to his Glory!

Letter from Charles Wesley to Sally Gwynne, written during their courtship

again till I do with my religion, and that I may never do *that* I am not ashamed to desire your prayers. 'Tis owing in great measure to somebody's (my mother's most likely) that I am come to think as I do, for I can't tell myself how or when I first awoke out of my lethargy—only that 'twas not long after you went away.

It was no easy matter to be religious in Oxford, however, and Charles longed for the haven which John had reached, writing on 5th January 1729 (in the first part of the letter which he completed on the 22nd):

My standing *here* is so very slippery, no wonder I long to shift my ground. Christ Church is certainly the worst place in the world to begin a reformation in. A man stands a very fair chance of being laughed out of his religion at his first setting out, in a place where 'tis scandalous to have any at all. Was the damning others the only means of saving themselves, they could scarce labour more heartily! I need say no more of them; you partly know them, and are got out of their cursed society: I wish to God I was, and shall be, I'm confident, when He sees it best for me!

Charles Wesley's spiritual awakening seems to have been at least partly influenced by the reaction from a mild love affair with a scheming actress, although he managed to resist the allurements of Molly and her mother:

To do the old lady justice she *did* give us opportunities enough, could I but have had the grace to ha' laid hold on them: and but for my strange College dullness Molly *might* have made something of me.... But hints were *lost* upon so dull, stupid a fellow as I was—and as such no doubt I have been since sufficiently laughed at.

When he wrote to John on 5th January 1729, however, the incident was over, for he had seen through Molly's make-up:

After all, I don't take her frailty much to heart, as I can without any regret resolve never to change another word

with the pretty creature; which I can the more easily refrain
from, as my eyes were partly opened by my last saving
journey to London; and I trust I shall keep them open, and
see the clearer by it, all the days of my life. One benefit I'm
sure to get by the bargain: from henceforth 'Peculiarem
habito nominem': I shall be far less addicted to gallantry,
and doing what sister Nutty with less justice said you did—
liking woman merely for being woman. . . . But enough
of her [i.e. Molly]—I'll blot my brain and paper no longer
with her.

Already Charles was a diligent student, spending much
time in 'collecting', or making extracts from the books
he read. In his studies, as in other matters, he followed
the example, and sought the advice, of his elder brother,
commencing the letter quoted above:

I have been so entirely taken up with my collections, that
I could not write sooner. At present I am head of the third
class, and shall be of the table this term, and then there will
be brave living for me! . . .
I can't take so long views as to foresee for a whole life;
but could manage a month perhaps or a year, and shall be
glad of your advice how I may make my best use of the
following. What I propose myself is to lay in a good stock
of Latin and Greek against I'm examined for my degree,
which at present terminates my prospect.

He knew himself less fitted by temperament for a life of
scholarship than John. The alertness of youth did not
make up for his inability to concentrate:

In my pursuit of knowledge I own I have this advantage of
you in some things. My brothers were born before me;
I start at twenty. But then I'm sure I'm less indebted to
nature than you. I'm very *desirous* of knowledge, but can't
bear the drudgery of coming at it near so well as you could.
In reading anything difficult, I'm bewildered in a much
shorter time than I believe you used to be at your first setting
out. My head will by no means keep pace with my heart, and
I'm afraid I shan't reconcile it in haste to the extraordinary
business of thinking.

He sought John's expert opinion in another matter:

I would willingly write a diary of my actions, but don't know how to go about it. What particulars am I to take notice of? Am I to give my thoughts and words, as well as deeds, a place in it? I'm to mark all the good and ill I do: and what besides? Must not I take account of my progress in learning as well as religion? What cipher can I make use of? If you would direct me to the same, or a like method with your own, I would gladly follow it, for I'm fully convinced of the usefulness of such an undertaking. I shall be at a stand till I hear from you.

Charles's letter to John on 5th May 1729 shows him fully launched on his task as an Oxford 'Methodist'. In writing it he used the abbreviated script which John himself employed—it is hardly a cipher, although it makes use of a few unusual symbols. Gone now was his careless gaiety, and his introspection and anxious striving after the good life are almost oppressive. His finger was constantly on his spiritual pulse:

What you say about coldness has put me upon considering whence mine can proceed, and how it may (be remedied?) I think I may truly esteem it the nature and just consequence of my past life. One who . . . has for almost thirteen years been utterly inattentive at public prayers can't expect to find there that warmth he has never known at his first seeking: he must knock oftener than once before 'tis opened to him: and is (I think) in some measure answerable for a heartlessness of which he himself is the cause.

Be that how it will, I resolve that my falling short of my duty in one particular shan't discourage me from vigorously prosecuting it in the rest. I look upon this coldness as a trial, and that unless I sink under it 'twill in the end greatly contribute to my advantage. I *must*, I *will*, in spite of Nature and the Devil, take pains: while my strength lasts, I *will* put it to the utmost stretch, for a day's relaxing throws me back to my first setting out. I won't give myself *leisure* to relapse, for I'm assured, if I have no business of my own, the Devil will soon find me some. You may show this if you think proper to my mother, for I would gladly have a letter from her upon this subject.

By rigid attention to the means of grace he trusted to earn spiritual salvation for himself. It was a grim struggle, however, with its defeats as well as its victories:

Last Saturday . . . I could not come home till eight at night: I then found myself utterly averse to prayer, and spent half an hour in vain striving to recollect my dissipated thoughts. Upon this I gave out, and passed the whole night in the utmost trouble and discomposure of mind. I rose in the morning two hours later than usual, in utter despair of receiving the Sacrament that day, or of recovering myself in less than two or three. In this condition I went immediately to church. On my way a thought came across me that it might be less sin to receive even without the least immediate preparation (for the whole week till Saturday evening I had spent to my satisfaction) than to turn my back upon the Sacrament. I accordingly resolved if I found myself anything affected with the prayers, to stay and communicate. I *did* find myself affected, and stayed. I not only received the Sacrament at that time with greater warmth than usual, but afterwards found my resolutions of pursuing considerably strengthened. This wasn't all: on Sunday night I received a great blessing from God, and have continued since in a better frame of mind than I have yet known. Dear brother, remember and pray for me when you receive this.

Charles Wesley was now gathering around him the nucleus of what was soon to be known as 'The Holy Club', whose origin he thus described in later years:

My first year at college I lost in diversions. The next I set myself to study. Diligence led me into serious thinking. I went to the weekly Sacrament, and persuaded two or three young scholars to accompany me, and to observe the method of study prescribed by the Statutes of the University. This gained me the harmless nickname of Methodist. In half a year my brother left his curacy at Epworth, and came to our assistance. We then proceeded regularly in our studies, and in doing what good we could to the bodies and souls of men.

His letter of 5th May 1729 introduced William Morgan, who with Robert Kirkham and Charles Wesley were the first 'Methodists':

Providence has at present put it in my power to do some
good. I have a modest, humble, well-disposed youth lives
next me, and have been (I thank God!) somewhat instrumental in keeping him so. He was got into vile hands, and is
now broke loose. I assisted in setting him free, and will do
my utmost to hinder his getting in with them again. He is
already content to live without any company but Bob's and
mine. He was of opinion that passive goodness was sufficient, and would fain have kept in with his acquaintance and God
at the same time. He durst not receive the Sacrament but
at the usual times for fear of being laughed at. I have persuaded him to neglect censure on a religious account, and
thereby greatly encouraged myself to do so. By convincing
him of the duty of frequent communication I have prevailed
on both of us to receive once a week. He has got Nelson
upon my recommendation, and is resolved to spare no pains
in working out his salvation.

Charles was far from happy about the third member of
the group, Robert Kirkham of Merton College, an old
friend whose chief merit in the eyes of the Wesley brothers
seems to have been that he was the brother of their 'dear
Varanese':

Would to God I could give you a like account of Bob! But
I'm afraid so he can but get to Heaven any way, the less
pains, he thinks, the better. I'm not uncharitable in my
opinion; you can't imagine how wretchedly lazy he is, and
how small a share of either learning or piety will content
him. Four hours a day he *will* spare for study out of his
diversions, not so many hours for diversions out of his studies!
What an excellent inverter! Nay and to my knowledge he is
not so scrupulous but half this will serve his turn at most times.

In his own zeal Charles even tried to deny himself the
sweet society of the ladies of Stanton rectory, replying
with some warmth to John's disillusioned words about
'Varanese', three years married to the Rev. Jack Chapone,
or Chapoon:

I'm so far from expecting but small satisfaction at Stanton,
that all I fear is meeting too much. Indeed I durst on no
account trust myself there without you, for as I take it strong

pleasure would be dangerous to one in my unconfirmed condition. They have had the good fortune there to have a couple of aunts die and leave the three girls £200 apiece: there's news for you, you rogue! I'm heartily glad for poor Bett and not a little for poor Damaris, because I believe it may help her to a husband the sooner. 'Tis well you at last own Sally not infallible—though she is so, I verily believe, for all your suspicions: all the business is, she is *not* changed, but Chapoon is Chapoon still.

Charles's sobered outlook was greeted at Westminster, in the summer of 1729, with some misgivings. In guarded language he wrote to John:

What my entertainment here has been I shan't say at present, though very welcome I was without doubt to my sister, for I have lost my stomach. There are so many and so surprising particulars in my reception, that I can tell you none of unless face to face—or at least you assure me I may do it with safety. If anything can prevent my ever disagreeing with you, 'twill be somebody's indignation that we agree so well. . . . They wonder here I'm so strangely dull (as indeed mirth and I have shook hands and parted), and at the same time pay the compliment of saying I grow extremely like you.

In spite of his phrase about bidding good-bye to mirth, Charles's gaiety never quite left him, and it was apt to bubble forth in moments of discomfort or danger. He was constantly making fun of his poverty. This particular journey from Epworth to London was made on foot in order to save expense, and Charles wrote:

I was seven days almost upon the road, and consequently had I not met with the luckiest company 'twas possible, should not now have had aught remaining of the nine shillings I brought into town with me. . . . There has been a Latin play acted at the College, with a farce at the tail on't for the entertainment of Prince William, who was present with half the nobility in town. . . . My Lord Charles' presence was wanting there, for many reasons a person of your sagacity may easily guess at—supposing for want of a coat or a shirt. Such accidents aren't the first of the kind his Lordship has met with at Westminster, though he may have the wit to say they shall be the last.

In November 1729 John Wesley returned from Lincolnshire to Oxford, to become the acknowledged leader of the religious study circle started by his brother. The following year Charles took his Bachelor's degree, and soon had a few pupils under his wing. They too were known as 'Methodists', for he not only gave them the benefit of his excellent knowledge of the classics, but introduced them also to the claims of personal religion, and of devout churchmanship. He was not always successful in his efforts, of course. In June 1731 he wrote to his father:

Since my return hither one of my pupils, Mr. Boyce, has taken his degree, but as I gave him all the assistance I could before I was paid for it, I shall continue to give it after. Another of them may do me good, though I can do him little. Our Censor has put it past my power from the time that he dissuaded him from weekly communion, monthly, as he assured him, being sufficient. One step farther indeed the young man has taken, and receives it now but thrice a year. Prayer and studying quickly followed the Sacrament, so that instead of an Enthusiast (as it was feared I should make him) I have got a hopeful young heathen to my pupil. My Gentleman-Commoner maintains his privilege of having no more religion than he has a fancy for, but my fourth pupil, the dullest rogue of them all, makes me sufficient amends, by being just what I would have him.

To the duty of frequent communion was later added that of fasting. In February 1733 he wrote to his brother Samuel:

Since my last I met with a remarkable clause in our Statutes, which not only justifies, but I think requires, my pressing the duty of fasting on my pupils.

He proceeded to quote the Statute in question, ending his letter with a veiled request for assistance in his graduation as M.A. on 12th March, which 'will cost ten pounds

—if you please'. Overleaf he sought the advice of his sister-in-law with regard to his gown:

Another important question I must beg to resolve is as to the price of prunella, whether it would not be the more saving way to buy the stuff at London, and have my gown made here. You'll be so good, too, when you write, . . . to let me know more particularly what effect rust and change of air (will have?)

Poverty continued to dog his footsteps. On 31st July 1734, writing to Samuel, who had become headmaster of Tiverton Grammar School, he said that he would gladly come over and help to get the garden in order were it not for 'want of time and money'. Playfully he added:

This is no hint, take notice; for when need be, you can bear witness to my proficiency in begging explicitly.

Six months later, however, he was on the point of selling the pictures from his study walls in order to buy clothing, though remarking:

if my shirts can but hold out till spring, my good friend Horn . . . has promised then to help me out a little.

Strangely enough, he did not canvass for pupils in order to meet his financial difficulties, writing to Samuel, 'if you have any pupils to send, pray send them to my brother', and by March 1735 he had only one left:

As to my title of 'tutor', I shall lose it with Dick Smith, unless Sam Bentham succeeds, whom I should be glad to take, and not sorry should he prove my last.

Epworth rectory seemed far away, though playful references to the ghost 'Jeffry' evinced a wistful homesickness. In his longing for news of home Charles could lose patience even with John, writing to Samuel:

I cannot excuse my brother's mentioning nothing of Epworth, when he was just come from it. Taciturnity as to family affairs is his infirmity, but not his fault, for I dare say there is no *malice prepense* in it. It was much he told me they were all well there; for he does not use to be so communicative.

That was in July 1734. The following March found the rector of Epworth very ill. Reluctantly Charles cancelled a proposed holiday with his brother Samuel:

This spring we hoped to have followed our inclinations to Tiverton, but are more loudly called another way. My father declines so fast, that before next year he will in all probability be at his journey's end; so that I must see him now, or never more with my bodily eyes. My mother seems more cast down at the apprehension of his death than I thought she could have been; and what is still worse, he seems so too.

The following sentence revealed Charles's ingrained filial respect. Though he had reached manhood's estate he still addressed his father as 'honoured sir', and would not criticize him to his face:

I wish I durst send him Hilarion's words of encouragement to his departing soul—'Go forth, my soul; what art thou now afraid of? Thou hast served thy God these threescore and ten years, and dost thou tremble now to appear before Him?' Methinks such a man as he should 'rejoice with joy unspeakable and full of glory' while he enters the haven, after such a succession of storms.

The rector of Epworth died on 25th April 1735, and Charles wrote Samuel a moving account of his last moments:

You have reason to envy us, who could attend him in the last stage of his illness. The few words he could utter I saved, and hope never to forget. . . . The fear of death he had entirely conquered, and at last gave up his latest human desires of finishing Job, paying his debts, and seeing you. He often laid his hand upon my head, and said 'Be steady. The Christian faith will surely revive in this kingdom; you shall see it, though I shall not.'

That dying prophecy was soon to be fulfilled.

CHAPTER II

AMERICAN INTERLUDE

The story of the Wesley brothers' mission to Georgia still needs much elucidation. Without doubt, however, it was for both John and Charles as much an attempt to find spiritual certainty for themselves as to proclaim the Gospel to the Red Indians. Charles was content to go as the lay shadow of his brother, as Oglethorpe's private secretary and also the official 'Secretary for Indian Affairs'. Brother John, however, would not be gainsaid. As Charles wrote to Dr. Chandler:

> I took my degrees, and only thought of spending all my days in Oxford. But my brother, who always had the ascendant over me, persuaded me to accompany him and Mr. Oglethorpe to Georgia. I exceedingly dreaded entering into Holy Orders, but he overruled me here also, and I was ordained deacon by the Bishop of Oxford, and the next Sunday priest by the Bishop of London.

Although Charles Wesley doubted whether he himself was 'renewed in the image of God', this did not prevent him from sending parting letters of spiritual admonition to young James Hutton. Hutton's home at Westminster adjoined that formerly occupied by Samuel Wesley, and here the brothers had lodged whilst waiting for their passage. The first letter was headed 'Gravesend, Oct. 19, 1735':

> The sadness you observed in me at our parting here was not on my own account, but yours. I feared that as soon as I was gone you would fold your arms again, and sink down into your spiritual lethargy, that nature would prevail over grace, and plunge you as deep as ever in that fatal lukewarmness which is more abominable with God than even sin itself.

The missionaries were delayed for some weeks, so that two further letters were sent. The first shows the passion of the evangelist already burning in Charles Wesley:

Might I presume to choose the way wherein God should reward [your parents] for all their good offices to me, it would be the making me the instrument of your salvation. My heart's desire to God for you is, that you may be saved; and 'tis worth my living and dying for this.

The second, written on 28th November, showed that brooding inactivity was not good for Charles's peace of mind:

I must add more, though I find no words to express myself. There is no writing down my sensations. I feel the weight and misery of my nature, and long to be freed from this body of corruptions.

When after two months at sea the *Simmonds* at length reached America, the black cloud of depression had settled thickly about him. Wistfully he thought of his past life. He pictured that choice little circle of female friends into which he had been introduced as an Oxford undergraduate—the Kirkhams and the Granvilles. He dwelt on the pleasant admixture of literary dalliance and religious musings, the playful secrecy of their pseudonyms, with himself disguised as 'Araspes', John as 'Cyrus', Mary Pendarves as 'Aspasia', and her younger sister Anne as 'Selima'. And above all he thought of Sally Kirkham, now securely married to the Rev. John Chapone—Sally Kirkham, the Wesleys' beloved 'Varanese'. Forgetting James Hutton, forgetting his brother Samuel, forgetting his mother, he poured out his soul to his 'first of friends, Varanese', a letter intended also for 'Selima', in which he said:

Besides you two, I have no relations, no friends in England, whom I either write to, or find any ease in thinking of. And for you I do pray continually, with an earnestness like that of Dives, that ye may never come into this state of torment.

The opening sentences of this long and important letter show how even the natural fears aroused by the beating of the terrible Atlantic storms on their fragile craft were as nothing compared with the emotions arising from his spiritual condition, his morbid fear that he was not wholly devoted to God, not accepted by Him:

> On board the Simmonds off the
> Island of Tibey in Georgia. Feb. 5. 1736

God has brought an unhappy, unthankful wretch hither, through a thousand dangers, to renew his complaints, and loathe the life which has been preserved by a series of miracles. I take the moment of my arrival to inform you of it, because I know you will thank Him, though I cannot. I cannot, for I yet feel myself. In vain have I fled from myself to America; I still groan under the intolerable weight of inherent misery! If I have never yet repented of my undertaking, it is because I could hope for nothing better in England—or Paradise. Go where I will, I carry my Hell about me. Nor have I the least ease in anything, unless in thinking of S[elima] and you.

Resolutely he turned from his own despair, however, to religious exhortation:

O that you both might profit by my loss, and never know the misery of divided affections. . . . I cannot follow my own advice, but yet I advise you—Give God your hearts; love Him with all your souls; serve Him with all your strength. Forget the things that are behind, riches, pleasure, honour—in a word, whatever does not lead to God. From this hour let your eye be single. Whatever ye speak, or think, or do, let God be your aim, and God only! . . . Think of nothing else. See nothing else. To love God, and to be beloved of Him, is enough.

As he wrote, his heart warmed. Of *their* salvation, at any rate, he was sure. Suddenly he realized that this buoyant enthusiasm was inconsistent with his opening sentences:

I cannot myself account for the strange expansion of heart which I feel in the midst of my wishes for your welfare. It is not charity, for that arises from the love of God, a principle I am utterly ignorant of. If it springs from ought else it is of no worth—and yet 'tis (all?) I have to rest my soul upon.

He had pulled himself down from the heights, and soon was in the depths again, as he mentioned his brother's journal:

He is indeed devoted. But I cannot bear to think of his happiness, and find a preposterous sort of joy that I am going to be removed from the sight of it. Could I hide me from myself too in these vast impervious forests, how gladly would I fly to 'em as my last asylum, and lose myself for ever in a blessed insensibility and forgetfulness! But it is a fruitless wish, and that salutation of Satan better becomes me—

> Hail, horrors, hail, and thou profoundest gloom
> Receive thy new possessor—one who brings
> A mind not to be changed by place or time![1]

A week or so later Charles Wesley picked up this letter again—in a better frame of mind, though still with the old gloom overshadowing him:

Feb. 14. off Peeper's Island.

My friends will rejoice with me in the interval of ease I at present enjoy. I look with horror back on the desperate spirit that dictated the words above, but shall let them stand, as the naked picture of a soul which can never know reserve toward you. I will still call myself a *Prisoner of Hope*. God is able to save, to the uttermost, to break my bonds in sunder, and bring deliverance to the captive! 'To what am I reserved?' is a question I am continually asking myself— though God alone can answer it. This, I am persuaded, will now be soon determined, for I am come to a crisis. The work I see immediately before me is the care of fifty poor families (alas for them that they should be so cared for!), some few of whom are not far from the Kingdom of God. Among these I shall either be converted or LOST. I need not ask your prayers; you both make mention of me in them continually. Obstinate pride, invincible sensuality, stand betwixt God and me. The whole bent of my soul is to be altered. My office calls for an ardent love of souls, a desire to spend and to be spent for them, an eagerness to lay down my life for the brethren. May the Spirit that maketh intercession for us, direct you how to intercede for me.

[1] Milton's *Paradise Lost*, I: 250–3, misquoted slightly.

When eventually on 9th March he set foot on St. Simon's Island in the south of Georgia, taking up his duties amongst the 'fifty poor families' of Frederica, the incubus of despair left him:

Immediately my spirit revived. No sooner did I enter upon my ministry than God gave me, like Saul, another heart.

Though inward conflicts were being stilled, however, his outward battles were but commencing. Like his brother John, he was soon the target for intriguing womenfolk, misunderstood, slandered, persecuted. A hint of this occurs in a letter to John, a letter probably carried north to Savannah by Benjamin Ingham. It is also important for the light it throws on religious conditions in Georgia, and on Charles's own spiritual progress:

Frederica, March 27th.

DEAR BROTHER,
I received your letter and box. My last to you was opened, the contents being publicly proclaimed by those who were so ungenerous as to intercept it. I have not yet complained to Mr. Oglethorpe. Though I trust I shall never either write or speak what I will not justify both to God and man, yet I would not have the secrets of my soul revealed to everyone. For their sakes, therefore, as well as for my own, I shall write no more, and desire you will not. . . .

Mr. Oglethorpe gave me an exceeding necessary piece of advice for you—'Beware of hypocrites, in particular of *log-house* converts.' They consider you as favoured by Mr. Oglethorpe, and will therefore put on the form of religion, to please—not God, but you. To this I shall only add, Give no temporal encouragement whatsoever to any seeming converts, else they will follow you for the sake of the loaves. Convince them thus, that it can never be worth their while to be hypocrites. . . .

God, you believe, has much work to do in America. I believe so too, and begin to enter into the designs which he has over *me*. I see why He brought me hither, and hope ere long to say with Ignatius, 'It is now that I *begin* to be a disciple of Christ.' God direct you to pray for me. Adieu.

Verse crept into his letters, in the shape of a poem later to be included in his first great publishing venture, the *Hymns and Sacred Poems* of 1749. To Mrs. Oglethorpe he wrote from Jekyl Island:

Last evening I wandered to the north end of the island, and stood upon the narrow point which your ladyship will recall as there projecting into the ocean. The vastness of the watery waste, as compared with my standing place, called to mind the briefness of human life and the immensity of its consequences, and my surroundings inspired me to write the enclosed hymn, beginning:

> Lo! on a narrow neck of land,
> 'Twixt two unbounded seas, I stand—

which, I trust, may pleasure your ladyship, weak and feeble as it is when compared with the songs of the sweet Psalmist of Israel.

His short stay in Frederica, however, seems to have had very few moments which could thus inspire him to verse. The rough and ready colonists disliked what they considered his intolerant piety. Their false accusations led to a misunderstanding with Oglethorpe. He contracted dysentery through lying on the bare ground, being prevented from buying boards to sleep on. He went down with fever. More and more it was being forced upon him that he was unfitted both physically and spiritually to be the pastor of this unruly Georgian flock. He began unburdening his mind to his neglected brother Samuel, maintaining in a letter of 8th April that he 'had lived eighteen years without God' (i.e. since he was a boy of ten). Although this gained Samuel's deserved rebuke, the following letters proved more acceptable, with their hints of a possible return to England, until Samuel wrote:

Yours from Savannah, May 15, is your last and best letter, because it brings news that you design to come back as soon as you can. The sooner the better, say I.

Charles Wesley's secretarial duties in Georgia do not seem to have been great, but he certainly did not enjoy them. Oglethorpe gave him the chance of honourable release, however, by making him the bearer of despatches to the Georgia Trustees in London. The first stage of his voyage was made both distasteful and perilous by a drunken captain, and he waited at Boston both for a more reliable boat and for recovery from his renewed illness. Whilst there, apparently at the home of Mr. Price, the friendly Boston commissary, he wrote to his brother John, who had accompanied him to Charlestown. His long letter of 5th and 6th October is interesting, not only for its contents, but because of its form. There had been so much trouble through intercepted letters that Charles was determined to avoid this danger, writing in a strange mixture of Latin, Greek, and shorthand. The only passage in English longhand read thus:

Oct. 6. If you are as desirous as I am of a correspondence, you must set upon Byrom's shorthand immediately. I leave my journal and other papers with Mr. Price, which he will send you if I fall short of England.[1]

The letter itself was full of unhappiness about the immediate past, and uncertainty about the future. The slanders and persecution of Georgia still rankled, even though he was not tender about his reputation, knowing his own conscience to be clear. Yet the general tone of the letter is one of calm resignation:

Dear Brother,
 I take (advantage?) of the deepest seriousness and best temper I have known since the fatal hour I left Oxford, to lay open my very heart, as I call God to witness that what I now write comes from it. You know what has passed in Georgia. . . . The snare is broken, and I am delivered by the only expedient that could have saved me. . . . I sometimes think how to dispose of the remainder of a (mad?) life.

[1] It was almost certainly owing to Charles's insistence that John Wesley at last took up Byrom's shorthand in earnest, on 20th December commencing its regular use in his own diary.

I can either live at Oxford or with my brother, who before I left England had provided for me without my asking. He will labour all he can to settle me. But I trust God will not suffer me to set up my rest there.[1]

Mentioning Mr. Price's offer of a comfortable church living either in Boston itself or in a small inland town, he continued:

But Georgia alone can give me the solitude I seek after. I cannot look for a long life there, but neither do I count that a blessing.

Meditative solitude was what he prized above everything else, Boston hospitality proving too much for him, though it was certainly in some particulars an improvement on Georgia:

I am wearied with this hospitable people, they so vex and tease me with their civilities. They do not suffer me to be alone. The clergy, who come from the country on a visit, drag me along with them when they return. I am constrained to take a view of this New England, more pleasant even than the old. I cannot help exclaiming, 'O happy country, that cherishes neither *flies*, nor *crocodiles*, nor *informers*'.

Illness was again disabling him, however:

My disorder, once removed by this most salubrious air, has again returned. All my friends advise me to consult a physician, but I cannot afford so expensive a funeral.[2]

On 15th October he told John, with a touch of the old despair:

I should be glad for your sake to give a satisfactory account of myself, but that you must never expect from me. It is fine talking while we have youth and health on our side; but sickness would spoil your boasting as well as mine. . . .

Though I am apt to think that I shall at length arrive in England to deliver what I am entrusted with, yet do I not expect, or wish for, a long life. How strong must the principle of self-preservation be, which can make such a wretch as I am willing to live at all!—Or rather unwilling to die;

[1] Transcribed from the shorthand. See p. 6.
[2] Translated from the Latin, as in Whitehead's *John Wesley*, i: 141–2.

for I know no greater pleasure in life, than in considering that it cannot last for ever. . . . I am just now much worse than ever; but nothing less than death shall hinder me from embarking.

On the 21st he wrote:

I am worried on all sides by the solicitations of my friends to defer my winter voyage till I have recovered a little strength. Mr. [Price?], I am apt to think, would allow me to wait a fortnight for the next ship: but then if I recover, my stay will be thought unnecessary. I must die to prove myself sick, and I can do no more at sea. I am therefore determined to be carried on board tomorrow, and leave the event to God.

On the 25th came his final note:

The ship fell down as was expected, but a contrary wind prevented me from following till now. At present I am something better: on board the *Hannah*, Captain Corney: in the state-room, which they have forced upon me. I have not strength for more.   Adieu.

And so Charles Wesley left America behind him, landing at Deal, after a storm-tossed voyage, on 3rd December 1736. For many weeks he was so ill that he was reported dead. Part of this time he was engaged in conversations about a closer union between the Moravians and Anglicans in Georgia—and was almost persuaded himself to seek Moravian retirement in Germany. Georgia still called, however. On 5th February 1737 he urged Oglethorpe, who had followed him to England, to arrange for his return—but as a minister this time, not as a secretary. He managed to visit 'Varanese', the Granvilles, the Huttons, his brother Samuel, and the rest of his relations. He spent much time in university circles, being chosen to present the Oxford Address to George II at Hampton Court. He talked his difficulties over with William Law at Putney, receiving the advice—'Renounce yourself: and be not impatient'.

The months passed by. Autumn drew on, and all the time Georgia was calling. Eventually the Trustees accepted him as a missionary, asking him to draw up plans for founding an orphan house in Georgia. It seemed that he would soon be braving once more the discomforts and dangers of the colony which had rejected him. His courage rose accordingly, for there was something of the martyr in his make-up. On 26th November 1737, he wrote in Latin to Count Zinzendorf:

After wandering through all the miseries of passion, I would fain turn at last to thee, to myself, and to God. . . . While I hung back and struggled, the Lord snatched me away and tore me with violence from my idol. In grief and despair I flung away the yoke of Christ defiantly, and lay for a long time in sin, having no hope and without God. At last, with difficulty and hesitation, I seem to be rising again. I would once more play the warrior, and force my way into freedom. May thy prayers and the prayers of the community at Herrnhut accompany me, and, I beg, may thy letters follow me, as I return to Georgia. Pray God on my behalf that I may be willing to be free, that I may thirst for Him alone, that I may fulfil my ministry.[1]

The letter then introduced a new name, that of one of the last students to be welcomed into the Holy Club by Charles Wesley, and one who was soon to take over the orphan house project from him:

I take with me a young man named George Whitefield, a minister of fervent spirit—if I may say so, a second Timothy. God has wonderfully aroused by his means the twice-dead populace. The churches will not contain the hearers. For indeed his word and his preaching is not in persuasive words of human wisdom but in the manifestation of the spirit and of power.

When on 29th November Charles Wesley told his mother of his plans, she 'vehemently protested'. Illness came to her support. Once more Charles was

[1] Translation by Drs. W. F. Lofthouse and Henry Bett.

incapacitated by dysentery. To George Whitefield's letter of inquiry he replied:

I could as soon fly as ride. . . . It makes no alteration in my designs: to go I am resolved on if anyone will set me on horseback and I can keep my seat. . . . Should I drop on the road and you sail before me, leave some money behind you with James [Hutton]. *. . . But it is not improbable I have a longer journey to go. Be that as it may. I have few attachments to this place, not many to leave.*

He did recover sufficiently to reach London on New Year's Eve, though by that time Whitefield was already on board the *Whitaker* at Gravesend. Before the ship set sail, however, Wesley managed to pay Whitefield a farewell visit, of which he gave an account on 2nd January 1738 to his brother John, whose troubled letters he had been reading:

Had I even resolved to have set up my rest here, your present trial would have broken my resolution, and forced me back to America, to partake with you in your sufferings for the Gospel. . . .

You remember the case of *Athanasius contra mundum*. The charge brought against him was worth bringing: treason, adultery, and murder, at once! I wonder no more is said against you. The devil himself could not wish for fitter instruments than those he actuates and inspires in Georgia. Whatever he will suggest, they will both say and swear to. . . . Here are many now who long to be partaker with you in the sufferings of the Gospel. I too would be of the number, and shall follow in sure and certain expectation of your treatment. The fiery furnace, I trust, will purify me; and if emptied of myself, I would defy the world and the devil to hurt me.

A note added to this letter on the 3rd was signed by six others of the little group gathered at Gravesend, in addition to Charles Wesley, George Whitefield, James Hutton, and Westley Hall.

For the time being illness had prevented Charles Wesley's renewed missionary venture. Even after his brother John's flight from Georgia, Charles was still determined to return. Another desperate illness followed, however, pleurisy this time, combined with violent neuralgia, which forced him to 'the abominable remedy of a pipe'. This put a final stop to the project. In March he dictated a letter to his brother Samuel:

DEAR BROTHER,
I borrow another's hand, as I cannot use my own. . . . [The doctors] bled me three times, and poured down draughts, oils, and apozems without end. For four days the balance was even. Then, as Spenser says,

    I over-wrestled my strong enemy.

Ever since I have been slowly gathering strength. . . .
One consequence of my sickness you will not be sorry for, its stopping my sudden return to Georgia. For the doctor tells me to undertake a voyage now would be certain death. Some reasons for *his* not going immediately my brother will mention to you in person.

To James Hutton he wrote in similar terms:

God has heard the prayers of my friends, and once more lifted me up from the gates of death. I am now walking about my room, and may venture out of it in a few days unless prevented by a relapse. The doctor tells me he expected at his second visit to have found me dead; that I must lay aside the thoughts of Georgia for some time at least, unless I would run upon certain death. If possible I must see the General [Oglethorpe] before he embarks.

The American interlude was over. On 3rd April 1738 he finally sent in his resignation as Secretary of Indian Affairs—delayed at Oglethorpe's request. Even as late as August 1739, however, he was writing wistfully to Whitefield, already setting out on his third Atlantic crossing:

I pray you all a good voyage, and that many poor souls may be added to the Church by your ministry before we meet again. Meet again I am confident we shall; perhaps both here and in America. The will of the Lord be done with us, and by us, in time and in eternity.

CHAPTER III

METHODIST PREACHER

CHARLES WESLEY's brief experience as a Christian missionary had not brought him the spiritual certainty for which he had hoped. Indirectly, however, it had taken him nearer his goal, by introducing him to the Moravians, and especially to Peter Böhler, a Moravian missionary himself on his way out to America. During the illness which put an end to Charles Wesley's own hopes of returning, Böhler visited him for English lessons, and took the opportunity of inquiring what reason his tutor had for hoping that he might be saved. When the invalid replied, 'Because I have used my best endeavours to serve God!', Böhler shook his head, and during later visits explained more fully the nature of justifying faith. Seeking to know more of this faith after Böhler had left, Wesley took up lodgings with John Bray in Little Britain. And there, on Whitsunday, 21st May 1738, the issue of his inner conflict was at last decided, and his journal recorded:

I now found myself at peace with God, and rejoiced in hope of loving Christ. . . . I saw that by faith I stood; by the continual support of faith, which kept me from falling, though of myself I am ever sinking into sin.

Two days later he was penning a hymn of praise in which he was shortly joined by his brother John:

> Where shall my wondering soul begin?
> How shall I all to heaven aspire?
> A slave redeemed from death and sin,
> A brand plucked from eternal fire,
> How shall I equal triumphs raise,
> Or sing my great Deliverer's praise?

A new life had begun for him. Depression was still to dog his footsteps, for it was one of the predominant traits of his volatile temperament. Nor did his longing for death vanish. It seemed, indeed, to increase at times, for 'to depart and to be with Christ' was 'far better'. The glowing certainty of 21st May 1738 lost some of its dazzling brilliance, and a note of doubt could be introduced into his later musings on the event:

Whitsunday, 1760. Westminster.
MY DEAREST SALLY,
This I once called the anniversary of my conversion. Just twenty-two years ago I thought I received the first grain of faith. But what does that avail me, if I have not the Spirit now? I account that the longsuffering of the Lord is salvation; and would fain believe, He has reserved me so long for good, and not for evil.

Henceforth, however, Whitsuntide was always to be a time of peculiar blessing for him. Underlying the choppy surface of his Christian experience were the calm deeps of his new certainty of God's love for him, a more confident reliance upon that love filling every moment of his life. Gone was the 'desperate spirit' which had dictated his letter from Georgia to 'Varanese'. There was a new enthusiasm, a new glow, a spiritual buoyancy which found its most lasting expression in the lilt of Christian song, but which also revealed itself in his letters.

Charles Wesley now had something about which he wanted to tell the world. Hitherto preaching had been a duty. Now it was a joy—or perhaps we should say an irresistible urge. To him, as to his brother John, addressing great crowds in the open air was a heavy cross, an affront both to his health, his temperament, and to his sense of ecclesiastical propriety. Yet he could not help himself. As he wrote to Whitefield in August 1739:

I am continually tempted to leave off preaching, and hide myself like J. Hutchins. I should then be freer from temptation, and at leisure to attend my own improvement. God continues to work *by* me, but not *in* me, that I can perceive. Do not reckon upon me, my brother, in the work God is doing: for I cannot expect He should long employ one who is ever longing and murmuring to be discharged.

Like all Methodist preachers, he was often called on to proclaim the message of salvation in strange places. In this he regarded himself as Whitefield's disciple, writing of preaching 'from George Whitefield's pulpit, the wall'. Loyal Churchman that he was, he rebelled against this unorthodox procedure even more than did his brother John, and even had scruples about preaching in the Huguenot Chapel at Spitalfields. Several times he debated whether he should escape by becoming a parish priest. When this question arose in 1740, he wrote to John for advice:

Heard that a C[hurch] living was vacant, which probably I might have the refusal of—or rather which I might be refused. Had a sudden thought whether I ought not to be refused it? to demonstrate it is no fault of mine that I do not preach within stone walls. B[rother] M[axfield], before I communicated my thoughts, had had the very same, and himself first mentioned them to me. In all probability neither will the canons present me, nor the bishop give me institution and induction. Should I not for this very reason offer myself, that they may be without excuse? What the living is, or where, I know not, I care not. Commend the matter to God, and send me your advice.

The living did not materialize, and he continued to preach in the open air, though with less reluctance. At Plymouth, for instance, in June 1746:

They desired me ... to preach in their society-house. I rather chose the street, having sent to the minister to desire the use of his church, which he civilly refused. A confused multitude were got together, and tolerably quiet, while I showed them the necessity of repentance and conversion. One blow I received on my head with a stone, for which my zealous friends the mob were ready to tear the poor man in pieces.

Many were come to hear me in hopes of my opposing Mr. Wh[itefiel]d, but were not a little disappointed at my confirming his saying, and bringing none other doctrine than salvation by grace through faith in Jesus. I gave notice of my intention to preach next evening in the same field where that faithful minister of Christ, my beloved brother G. Wh[itefiel]d, had first showed them the way of salvation.

As can be seen, Charles Wesley did not escape his share of persecution. Nor did he flinch from it. In fact it seemed to fire him to greater enthusiasm. On this same visit to Plymouth the rabble which endeavoured to break up his meeting, and thus drive him away in terror, achieved exactly the opposite:

I then gave notice that I should not depart on the morrow as I proposed, but stay a few days with them, seeing the Enemy was so alarmed; and warned the opposers not to be too violent, lest I should stay to live and die with them.

Perhaps one of the strangest reactions to physical violence ever recorded is to be found in his letter describing an interview with Henry Seward in March 1740:

'Rogue, rascal, villain, pickpocket,' were all the titles he could afford me. He acknowledged his putting the pistols into his pocket, only to frighten me, he said, but now he justified it, and insisted I ought to be shot through the head . . . [I said that] it might sometimes be well to answer a fool according to his folly. *Henry started up, and most courageously pulled me by the nose.*[1] The cries of Mrs. S[eward] stopped any further violence. I was immediately filled with inexpressible comfort; sat still, and felt the hand of God upon me; had not the least temptation to anger or fear; said with perfect calmness to Mrs. S[eward], 'Be not disquieted, madam, upon my account; I have learned to turn the other cheek'; opened a Testament upon those words 'Jesus wept', and broke out with B[rother] M[axfield?] into 'Praise God from whom all blessings flow!'

In spite of his reserve, Charles Wesley was a born preacher. It is a significant fact that the most frequently

[1] Not shorthand, but underlined in the original. See note, p. 6.

published Methodist pamphlet was a sermon by Charles Wesley—*Awake, thou that sleepest*. One of his greatest thrills, and greatest temptations, was that of feeling a huge crowd responding to his own emotions, as at Runwick in August 1739:

The minister here lent me his pulpit. I stood at the window (which was taken down), and turned to the larger congregation of above two thousand in the churchyard. They appeared greedy to hear, while I testified 'God so loved the world, that He gave His only-begotten Son.' . . .

In the afternoon . . . the church was full as it could crowd. Thousands stood in the churchyard. It was the most beautiful sight I ever beheld. The people filled the gradually rising area, which was shut up on three sides by a vast perpendicular hill. On the top and bottom of this hill was a circular row of trees. In this amphitheatre they stood, deeply attentive, while I called upon them in Christ's words, 'Come unto Me, all that are weary'. The tears of many testified that they were ready to enter into that rest. God enabled me to lift up my voice like a trumpet, so that all distinctly heard me. I concluded with singing an invitation to sinners.

We are reminded by the last sentence that he had a fine voice for singing, as well as for preaching. It is good to think of him underlining his evangelical appeal by the singing of his own verses—'O let me commend my Saviour to you'; 'O all that pass by, to Jesus draw near'; or 'Would Jesus have the sinner die?'

Unlike his calmly reasoning brother, Charles was often carried away by his emotions. Yet he also looked askance at the cruder emotional outbursts so common to religious revivals. About the phenomena at Bristol in 1740 he wrote to his brother:

The noises and outcries here are over. I have not spoken one word against them, nor two *about* them. The Devil grows sullen and dumb, because we take no notice of him.

The vehemence and length of Charles Wesley's preaching frequently proved too much of a tax for his fine voice.

In his early days his sermons on occasion lasted as long as two hours. Even as late as 1764 he wrote:

My subject at Spitalfields—'The eternal God is thy refuge, and underneath are the everlasting arms'. . . . From hence I strongly preached the great salvation. . . . It should seem I spoke as the oracles of God, by the abundant testimony He gave to the word of His grace. For near an hour he opened my mouth to declare the mystery of the gospel, so as I have seldom spoken. A thousand hearers, I believe, would have ventured their lives on the truth of my report. . . .

I have blamed Mr. Venn for his long sermon, and at the Foundery I preached one of near an hour and an half long to above five thousand listening souls. (Five or six hundred more it is supposed to hold since the alterations.) My subject was 'Ho, every one that thirsteth, come ye to the waters'. I was much drawn out, you may suppose, by my keeping the people so long. Never was I assisted more. Give God the glory.

Throughout his life Charles Wesley's preaching was practically confined to the central truths of the gospel of redemption. Even after the close of his journal proper the miniature journals which he wrote in letters to his wife abounded with details such as these:

On Sunday my subject was Isai. 61. 1, 'The Spirit of the Lord God is upon me, &c.' He gave testimony to the word.

I preached on Friday from Rom. 5. 10, 'If while we were enemies &c.' Never with greater enlargement.

Age made a difference, though even when nearing eighty he could write:

Monday, Aug. 8, 1785. . . . My subject yesterday was 'God be merciful to me a sinner.' . . . Wedn. Morn. . . . Wherever I go, I hear of the blessings received [on] Sunday. It was one of the old gospel-days. . . . [Thursday.] Preached at night, 'Be ye also ready'—an old Methodist sermon.

Charles Wesley had a few favourite sermons, and even toyed with the idea, urged on him by his friends, of printing them. He was a great believer in spontaneity, however, so that his manuscript sermons were comparatively few.[1] Good Churchman though he was, he was continually discarding his *Book of Common Prayer* and praying extempore—praying '*after* God' as he called it. His preaching partook of the same character. It was in October 1738 that he had first ventured to preach extempore, in St. Antholin's Church, Bristol, when he 'spoke on justification, from Romans iii, for three quarters of an hour without hesitation'. The method which he seems to have preferred in these early days was not to prepare any sermon at all, but simply to leave the matter to the inspiration of the moment. Thus he wrote to his brother John in March 1740:

I was greatly distracted by an unusual unnecessary premeditating what to preach upon. My late discourses had worked different effects. Some were wounded, some hardened and scandalized above measure. I hear of no neuters. The Word has turned them upside down. In the pulpit, I opened the book and found the place where it was written, 'The Spirit of the Lord is upon me, because He hath anointed me to preach the gospel to the poor, &c.' I explained our Lord's prophetic office, and described the persons on whom alone He could perform it. I found as did others that He owned me.

Throughout his life Charles Wesley kept up the practice of opening his Bible and reading the first sentence which presented itself as God's message either for his own personal problem or, at least occasionally, for the needs of a waiting congregation. We remember, of course, that in his case this type of sermon preparation was not as dangerous as it would be for most people, for he knew the Scriptures as few have done, and at whatever page he opened he was almost certain to find himself on

---

[1] 130 sermons and outlines are preserved in the Colman Collection at the Methodist Book Room.

familiar ground. Even more than his brother John he was a man of one book—the Bible. His hymns contain reminiscences of Scripture in almost every line. So it is with many of his letters, especially those of exhortation, which afford us clear examples of his Bible-saturated preaching style. Here is one chosen at random:

Newcastle, Dec. 11, 1746.

'This is the victory that overcometh the world, even our faith'; and I *shall* hear my dear friend Blackwell say, 'Thanks be to God, who giveth *me* the victory through *my* Lord Jesus Christ'. . . . Cannot you hear Him say this moment, 'Zaccheus, make haste and come down; for to-day I must abide at thy house?' O receive, receive Him gladly, while He comes to be guest with a man that is a sinner! You are not indeed worthy that He should come under your roof; neither can you ever prepare your own heart to admit Him. All you can do is, not to hinder; not to keep Him out, by willingly harbouring any of His enemies, such as worldly, proud, or angry thoughts or designs. . . . His work is before Him. Every valley shall be exalted, (all the abjectness of your unbelieving heart,) and every mountain and hill made low, (all the haughtiness and pride of your spirit,) and the crooked shall be made straight, (your crooked, perverse will,) and the rough places plain, (your rugged, uneven temper,) and *then* the glory of the Lord shall be revealed, and we all shall see it together; for the mouth of the Lord hath spoken it.

The detailed working out of Biblical allegory seems to have been a prominent feature of Charles Wesley's preaching, his poetic imagination thus colouring his sermons. This is illustrated by a letter describing a sermon on one of his favourite subjects:

I read prayers, and preached the *pure Gospel* from the Good Samaritan. Surely He was in the midst of us, pouring in His oil. Some seemed ready for Him; and it cannot be long before He binds up their wounds, and brings them into His inn, and takes care of them. He gave money to me the host that I too might take care of His patients. I was greatly concerned for their recovery.

Charles Wesley's neglect of active preparation for preaching is an example of that exaggerated distrust of human effort into which those who have thrown themselves utterly on God's resources have sometimes been betrayed. For a time at least he was in danger of forsaking all active religion, and succumbing to the appeal of 'stillness'—the complete renunciation of human effort along the pathway to salvation, and the denial of any real value in the so-called means of grace. The year 1740 found many Methodists in grave spiritual danger from the handful of Moravians who insisted on such an approach to religion. At first Charles was firmly with his brother against this teaching, his strong views finding their way into his sermons despite his resolutions to the contrary. On Easter Day he preached at the Foundery, London, sending the following report to John:

I strongly preached Christ and the power of His resurrection from Phil. iii. 9, 10. My intention was not to mention one word of the controverted points till I had spoken with each of those who had troubled Christ's little ones. But God ordered it better. He led me, I know not how, in ipsam aciem et certamen.[1] How or where it came in I cannot conceive, but my mouth was opened, and the Spirit gave me utterance as I never before experienced. I asked, 'Who hath bewitched you that you should let go your Saviour? that you should cast away your shield and your confidence, and deny you ever knew Him?' Somewhat like this (I don't well know what) I said, and there followed such a burst of sorrow as you never saw. Brother Maxfield has the full strong witness in himself. Near one thousand, he says, were melted into tears.

During the following winter, however, he became more and more enamoured of the prospect of retirement from the world amongst the Moravians, and on 28th February 1741 wrote to his brother:

[1] A rough translation is: 'into the very front line of battle'.

Perhaps you may see me next week in B[ristol]: but speak not of it, for 'tis only a perhaps—perhaps I may go with B[öhler] to G[ermany?].

If you are shortly left alone, take notice beforehand that I do not depart by reason of any alteration of my judgment (much less affection), but merely through weakness both of soul and body. I wish you good luck in the name of the Lord. May His pleasure and work prosper in your hand.

To the end of his life Charles remained in closer sympathy with the Moravians than did his brother, and continued to discuss the possibilities of reunion with them. Their influence over him at this period waned, however, when he found himself in the thick of a theological controversy with his former comrade, George Whitefield. Resolutely he took his stand with John Wesley against Whitefield's Calvinism, writing on 16th March 1741:

Mon.

Dear Brother,[1]

By the time this reaches Bristol, I suppose you will be at London; but if you should not be set out, this is to summon you hither immediately.

George Whitefield, you know, is come.[2] His fair words are not to be trusted to; for his actions show most unfriendly. An answer to your sermon he just put into my hands. The title was enough. I endorsed it 'Put up again thy sword into its place', and deferred reading, till it is in print. . . .

Tu. Morn.

G. W. came into the desk, while I was showing the believer's privilege, i.e. power over sin. After speaking something, I desired him to preach. He did—predestination, perseverance, and the necessity of sinning. Afterwards I mildly expostulated with him, asking if he would commend me for preaching the opposite doctrines in his Orphan-house, protesting against the publishing his answer to you, and labouring for peace to the utmost of my power.

---

[1] Charles Wesley usually commenced his letters to John with the shorthand characters, 'Dr B'.

[2] Transcribed from the shorthand. See note, p. 6.

His own spiritual turmoil was not quite forgotten, however:

> I am marvellously unconcerned at the prospect of the storm and distraction that must surely follow. My soul is otherwise taken up ... I am struggling in the toils of death:
> > Who shall tell me if the strife
> > In Heaven or Hell shall end?

Soon this period of distress was over, and Charles Wesley was once more preaching up and down the English countryside, and especially in the great centres of population. Undermined by his early privations and sufferings, his health gradually gave way under the physical strain of this heavy routine, though he bravely attempted to shoulder the burden to the end. In March 1771 he wrote from London:

> On Sunday at nine word was brought me that Mr. Richardson had had a second fit and could not assist me. I was forced therefore to go through the whole service, sermon, and Sacrament to five hundred, alone. Had scarce time to dine before I was called to repeat the same. In preaching, every word went to my heart, but I did not fully feel my fatigue till afterwards—was full of stitches and pains all night. My old pain is returned, and seems fixed in my breast. I hope it will be dislodged by Sunday. Till then I lie by.
>
> I thought of G. Whitefield's last sermon of two hours, and should not repent of Sunday, if it finished my work. However, I shall never more attempt so much at a time.

Yet in the summer of 1787, when he was nearing eighty, he still managed to preach twice each Sunday.

To physical weakness, temperamental shrinking and depression, misunderstanding and persecution, were added, of course, the difficulties of travel. The life of an itinerant preacher in the eighteenth century was a hard one indeed, a hint of which we see in a letter written from Gloucester in August 1739:

> By ten last night the Lord brought us hither through many dangers and difficulties. In mounting, I fell over my horse,

and sprained my hand. Riding in the dark, I bruised my foot. We lost our way as often as we could. Two horses we had between three.

Even some of the main roads were then little more than cart tracks, and conditions on the cross roads passed imagination—wheel-deep with mire in wet weather, in the dry season a succession of ruts and pitfalls for the unwary traveller. Under such conditions, the additional hazards of storms and highwaymen made a lone journey along deserted roads a real adventure, calling for great courage and resolution. There is a world of meaning for the sympathetic reader in a simple sentence such as this:

The roads are full of rain and robbers. My horse could scarce keep his legs, or I the saddle, in coming hither. It blew an hurricane.

On this very occasion, however, Charles Wesley managed to laugh at his troubles, saying 'we had only one shower—but it lasted from morning to night'. Nor was he one to take the easy path. This is revealed in a letter of 1749:

Before five this morning I took horse for Shoreham, though the waters were out still, and higher than when I passed them last, and I should have them to pass in the dark. . . . I soon reached Shoreham, having gone a little out of my way to avoid danger (the first time that I remember) by the advice of the turnpike man.

It is only in the light of contemporary conditions of travelling that we can appreciate the tremendous labours of that prince of itinerants, John Wesley. Nor was his brother Charles far behind, at least during the first half of his fifty years as a Methodist preacher. For nearly a decade his labours were confined to England. But the headings of his letters reveal the wide extent of his journeys. The mere handful preserved for the year 1746, for instance, were addressed from places as far apart as London, Bristol, St. Ives, Plymouth, and Newcastle. The following year a new name was to be added—Dublin.

CHAPTER IV

DUBLIN'S FAIR CITY

THE repercussions of the planting of Methodism in Ireland have been far more important than could have been realized at the time. Apart from the influence on Ireland itself, the influx of virile Irish blood into English Methodism has been noteworthy, from the days of that converted Roman Catholic Thomas Walsh and of Adam Clarke, down to our own times. Most important of all, however, has been the contribution to world Methodism through the stream of emigrants who carried their Methodist experience along with them as their most treasured possession. Newfoundland, Canada, the West Indies, and more particularly the United States of America, were evangelized by Irish pioneers. When, therefore, John Wesley stepped ashore at Dublin on 9th August 1747, on the first of his twenty-one lengthy visits, he was inaugurating a new era. But the influence of his brother Charles in the formative opening period must not be overlooked.

Realizing that he himself could not remain long enough to see the Dublin Methodists securely settled, John Wesley sent two urgent messages to his brother. On 9th September 1747 Charles arrived in Dublin, to find the embryo society almost shattered by persecution. He was soon in the thick of the fray. A few days later he wrote to his banker friend Ebenezer Blackwell, enclosing the foolscap pages of his journal, which since his Georgia days had accompanied letters to his friends:

Dublin, Sept. 17.
DEAR SIR,
Can you stand safe on shore, and see us in the ship, tossed with tempest, and not pity us? Let your compassion put you

to constant prayer for the little persecuted flock in this place. We live literally by (the prayer of) faith. The journal contains a few particulars. Please to let my brother have it when read.

Here are very many who long to hear the Word but are kept away by fear. Neither is their fear groundless, for unless the jury find the bill against the rioters murder there will surely be: and if it begin, it will not end, with us.

I cannot repent of my coming hither in such a dangerous season; nor am I anxious about the court. The hairs of my head are all numbered, and if my Master has more work for me, I shall certainly live to do it.

On the same day he sent a letter even more full of foreboding—this time to Sally Gwynne, the third daughter of Marmaduke Gwynne, a Welsh magistrate converted to Methodism by the preaching of Howell Harris. It is his first extant letter (unfortunately defective) to the one who was shortly to become his bride. She was nearing her twenty-first birthday: he was almost forty:

I shall probably see you sooner than I expected in G[arth]. God is still able to deliver His servants out of the(ir trouble?). That He can, I know: that He *will*, is hid from (me. Perhaps it would?) be best that my useless warfare should end here. (I go daily?) through this city amidst the curses and threatenings (of fierce and ma?)ny enemies. That line is continually (in my thoughts:?)

'Take the sad life, which I have long disda(ined &c.'

Whe?)ther I carry it a few days longer, or now lay down my burden, my spirit rejoices in sure and stedfast hope of meeting you where the wicked cease from troubling, where the weary are at rest!

The tide turned. On 10th October he wrote to Blackwell:

At my first coming here, I may truly say, 'No man stood with me; notwithstanding, the Lord stood with me.' We were so persecuted, that no one in Dublin would venture to let us an house or a room; but now their hearts are turned, as in a moment, and we have the offer of several convenient places.

The exhilaration caused by the imminence of danger forsook him, and he had time to ponder on his physical discomfort, confessing to his brother how much he looked forward to the new surroundings at Dolphin's Barn, made possible by this sudden rise in public favour:

I must go there or to some other lodgings, or take my flight. For here I can stay no longer. A family of squalling children, a landlady just ready to lie in, a maid who has no time to do the least thing for us, are some of our conveniences. Our two rooms for four persons (six when J. Healy and J. Haughton come) allow no opportunity for retirement. Charles [Perronet] and I groan for elbow-room; our diet answerable to our lodgings; no one to mend our clothes; no money to buy more. I marvel that we have stood our ground so long in these lamentable circumstances. It is well I could not foresee while on your side of the water.

From his new-found security he wrote:

Dolphin's Barn. Oct. 13.
Dear Brother,
This is a dangerous place: so quiet and retired I could hide myself here of *my* time. . . . 'Tis thousand pities to spoil this pretty house and garden. You shall *have it for your own, if Mr. Clark does not choose it: but you must send me money to pay for it, if it be not sent already. The bill I have received, and spent before it came, upon* myself and companion. His money, and three guineas of Trembath's, and book-money borrowed, and five guineas, and four given me for printing, are to be paid out of it—besides money for keeping our horses two months, and two persons' travelling expenses to Bristol with the horses. All which I must furnish out of my £20, so that I don't expect so many shillings surplus. J. Trembath (and Chas. Perronet most probably) will leave us Oct. 26. . . .
I do not care to tell you, lest it should not last, but I have more life of late than for a long time past.
Farewell.

Not that all his troubles were over, of course. The journal-letter for Sunday, 25th October, with its unflattering references to Dean Swift's cathedral, reveals that, as well as giving a typical picture of Charles Wesley's labours in Dublin:

Passed three hours under my usual burden, among the dry bones of the house of Israel—at St. Patrick's, I mean, in public prayer and the Sacrament. How different the spirit here from that in our chapel at London! I seldom enter this place but the zealots are ready to drag me out, like that old profaner of the temple, Paul. Such murmuring, disputing, railing, and loud abuse the very sight of me occasions, that I can compare the house of God to nothing but a den of thieves and murderers. The Dean [Francis Corbet] indeed I must except, and give honour to whom honour is due. He has always behaved towards us with great courtesy and love; looks pleased to see us make the bulk of the communicants; appointed us a seat for ourselves (but the underling officers soon thrust us out); and constantly administers the Sacrament to me first, as the order of our Church requires.

Stood our ground in the Green for half an hour, in the rain. Gave the Sacrament to a poor dying youth, who seems not far from the blood of sprinkling. Went to church at St. Catherine's, and walked thence, at half hour past five, in the cark and dirt to Dolphin's Barn. Mr. Perronet had by mistake given notice of my preaching there *after* evening service. I should never have chosen to *begin*[1] in the night, and before our windows were secured by shutters, but was now compelled to it, sorely against my will. The house, I found, would not hold a quarter of the congregation, and therefore stood in the garden, under the house-wall. Between one and two thousand stood in the open air, and drank in the strange glad tidings. . . .

J. Trembath was preaching at the same time to a yard full of serious hearers in Mary-bone Lane. We met, soon after seven, at our lodgings. I expected the society only; but hundreds were crammed together in all the room and stairs to hear the Word. I was quite exhausted with preaching four times to-day already, and walking several miles; but the Lord gave me fresh strength to expound His meeting with Zacchaeus. I feared one of our lodgers, a Papist, would be offended, but he was wonderfully pleased, and many others comforted together with me. Our brother Verney especially, who could truly say, 'This day is salvation come to this house!'

[1] This was the opening service at Dolphin's Barn.

It was near nine before the company went; and then I found myself as fresh and strong as in the morning.

The more personal note to John Wesley with which this journal closed, a note almost wholly in shorthand, reveals the rather unsatisfactory characters of the pioneer lay preachers in Ireland, which made all the more necessary an extension of Charles Wesley's visit:

J. Trembath must stay with me. It is as much as his soul is worth to be left to himself till he is humbled so far as to see his danger.

Haughton I don't expect to see before our brethren go hence. 'Twas inexcusable, his delay, when you wrote me word from Dublin that you had *then* sent him orders to set out. . . .

We propose building a kind of booth in our garden to screen the hearers this winter. . . . I set up my rest here for the winter. Toward February, I presume, you will relieve me yourself. *Mr. Williams is running into debt again: but take no notice of it to him. If my warning will stop him, well: if not, that will only happen which I expect, and we must part again. It cannot yet enter into my heart to conceive that God will ever join him and me in one work.*

Charles went on to protest against binding himself to follow his brother's example in giving up tea, ending:

However, my example need not clash with yours. We are on different sides of the water, and may so continue. I am very well content to give up old England, and see it no more for ever. But if we should meet there again, my present mind is to abstain from tea there, merely to oblige.

The above journal send to Mr. Blackwell and Mr. Perronet. Peace be with you.

Dublin, Oct. 29. *Farewell.*

On the same day he wrote also to Blackwell, his letter showing a little of that uncertainty (which never left him) as to whether John Wesley would think it worth while to carry out his requests:

If my brother does not send you my journals, as soon as he has read them, let me know, and I will transmit them to him through your hands.

It is in a letter to Ebenezer Blackwell later in the year, on 15th December 1747, that we read of the great progress made during Charles Wesley's prolonged stay in Dublin. So thoroughly established was the work that fresh ground could be broken farther afield:

We sent forth a preacher last week into the country about forty miles from Dublin, who sends us news that the Word of the Lord runs very swiftly among them, and there is a promise of a glorious harvest. . . .
In the beginning of the spring I shall begin to look towards England; but this people will not let me go, unless you send my brother in exchange.

In February 1748 Charles Wesley himself penetrated inland, to Tyrell's Pass and on to Athlone, near which latter place he and his companions were ambushed, and narrowly escaped with their lives.

John Wesley came to Charles's relief in March 1748, following up the new ventures that had been started. The 1748 Conference kept them both away from Ireland for a time, but Charles's self-sacrificing six months had laid a secure foundation. In August he was back again, consolidating the pioneer work of Thomas Williams and Robert Swindells at Cork, and doing a little pioneering on his own. He wrote to Blackwell:

Kinsale, Sept. 8, 1748.
MY DEAR FRIEND AND BROTHER,
Rejoice with me, for I have found the sheep that was lost—and not one only, but a whole flock. The harvest truly is plenteous; and these fields are white unto the harvest. High and low, rich and poor, *approve*, and many *taste*, the good word of grace.
This place was fallow ground. I preached yesterday for the first time, and cried again in the market-place, 'Ho! every one that thirsteth, come ye to the waters!' This morning God struck the hard rock, and the waters flowed. Follow us with your prayers, that in every place the word may have free course, and God may be glorified in the conversion of sinners.

I passed three days of this week at Bandon, a large town of all Protestants, and they all stretched out their hands unto the pardoning God. Cork is all on fire for and with the Gospel. Multitudes would there be added to the Church, if we had but a place to preach in. The weather will quickly drive us out of the field, but we have no winter quarters. A friendly Quaker offers us ground to build on. Our well-wishers have begun a subscription. *Your* vote and interest is desired. And, pray, pack up my brother also, and send him by the first ship.

On Monday se'nnight I propose to leave Cork and travel through the country societies to Dublin; and thence through Wales to London.

His farewell to the Cork Methodists on 18th September —his final farewell, though he did not realize it then— was an occasion of great emotion, which he thus described to Sally Gwynne:

Sun. Night.—This has been a day of trial and pain. I almost despaired of being able to open my mouth or take my leave of this dearest people. Yet at five I went forth to an innumerable multitude, and the Lord astonished me with the power He gave me. Never have I been more drawn out in prayer and preaching. For two hours I spake with a trumpet voice, and the hearts of all were bowed before the Lord, who gave testimony to His Word. My pain and weakness is all gone. I have forced my way through the weeping flock, to finish this. The Lord Jesus give you a share of the innumerable blessings but now showered down upon me by His people. I cannot now doubt of my prosperous journey. Faith laughs at impossibilities.

Less than a month later he was saying good-bye to his friends in Dublin also, and saying good-bye with a sense of imminent danger. The letter informing his Dublin host, Mr. Lunell, of his safe arrival at Holyhead on 10th October breathed surprise as well as fervent gratitude to God:

MY VERY DEAR FRIEND AND BROTHER,

I did not tell you what I felt at leaving you, but never had I a stronger apprehension of evil near. These sort of bodings or presages I rarely speak of, till after their confirmation. On Saturday evening, half hour past eight, I entered the smallboat. We were two hours making our way through the calm and fog to the vessel at the piles. There was not then water to cross the bar, so we took our rest till eleven on Sunday morning. Then God sent us a fair wind out of His treasuries, and we sailed smoothly before it at five knots an hour. All things promised a speedy, prosperous voyage, yet still I found the *usual* burden upon my heart—usual, I mean, in time of extreme danger approaching.

Toward evening the wind freshened upon us, and we had full enough of it. I was called to account for a bit of cake I ate in the morning, and [was] thrown into violent exercise. The emptiness of my stomach made it so much the worse. All my sickness in my voyage to America &c were nothing like this. I expected it would throw me into convulsions. Up or down, cabin or deck, made no difference. Yet in the midst of it I perceived a distinct and heavier concern, for I knew not what.

'Twas now pitch dark, so that we could not see the Head, and no small tempest lay upon us. The captain had ordered in all the sails. I kept mostly upon deck till half hour past eight, when upon my inquiry he told me he expected to be in the harbour by nine. I answered, we would compound for ten. While we were talking, the mainsail (as I take it) got loose and flew overboard, as if it would drag us all after it. The small-boat at the same time, for want of fastening, fell out of its place. The master called 'All hands upon deck!' and thrust me down into the cabin. Within a minute I heard a cry above, 'We have lost the mast!' A passenger ran up and brought us worse news, that it was not the mast, but the poor master himself, whom I had scarce left when the boat, as they supposed, struck him overboard—but from that moment he was neither seen nor heard more. My soul was bowed before the Lord. I knelt down and commended his departing spirit to His mercy in Christ Jesus. I adored His distinguishing goodness—'The one shall be taken and the other left.' Why was not I rather than that poor soul so hurried into eternity without a moment's notice? It brought into my mind those lines of Young which I had read this morning:

> No warning given, unceremonious fate!
> A sudden rush from life's meridian joys,
> A plunge opaque beyond conjecture.

The sailors were so hurried and confounded they knew not what they did. I thought it well for us that Jesus was at the helm. The decks were strewed with sails, boat, &c; the wind shifting about; the compass they could not get at, no nor the helm for some time. We were just on the shore, and the vessel drove, where or how they knew not. One of our cabin passengers ran to the helm, gave orders as captain, and was very helpful in righting the ship. But I ascribe it to our invisible pilot that we got safe to the harbour, soon after ten.

His gratitude found expression in a poem, appended to his letter:

THANKSGIVING FOR OUR DELIVERANCE FROM SHIPWRECK

1.   All praise to the Lord
    Who rules with a word
    The untractable sea,
And limits its rage by His stedfast decree.
    Whose providence binds
    Or releases the winds,
    And compels them again
At His beck to put on the invisible chain.

2.   Ev'n now He hath heard
    Our cry, and appeared
    On the face of the deep,
And commanded the tempest its distance to keep;
    His piloting hand
    Hath brought us to land,
    And no longer distressed
We are joyful again in the haven to rest. . . .

It was a fitting close to a short but effectual ministry, which bore rich fruit. Irish Methodism was now securely established, so that the terrible persecutions which were soon to follow at Cork failed in their aim of scattering the Methodists. Charles Wesley continued anxiously to follow their progress from England. A few weeks after his remarkable escape he wrote the following brief note, apparently from Bristol, to a London Moravian, William Holland:

My dear brother,

The Lord hath done great things for us already, whereof we rejoice. Surely He has much people in Ireland. If we could but bind those priests of Baal, a nation might be born in a day. Yet in spite of all opposition, we pick up every day more lost sheep of the Romish communion. Remember them, and me. I hope to see you ere long.

Here also is a living, growing people, and in all the country round.

Farewell.

The following February he wrote to Joseph Cownley, stationed in Dublin:

It would be a great satisfaction to me to see my dear friends on that side of the water: but God's time is not yet. My kindest love and blessing to all our children in the gospel.

On 9th April he repeated this sentiment:

My kindest love to our dear friends in Ireland, whom I should greatly rejoice to see.

Something had happened the previous day, however, which probably more than anything else prevented his ever fulfilling that hope of revisiting his spiritual children in Ireland. On 8th April 1749 he had married Sally Gwynne.

CHAPTER V

SALLY GWYNNE

DURING Charles Wesley's closing interview with General Oglethorpe in Georgia, the General had said:

On many accounts I should recommend to you marriage rather than celibacy. You are of a social temper, and would find in a married state the difficulties of working out your salvation exceedingly lessened, and your helps as much increased.

This seems to have been sound psychology. Charles Wesley, however, was one of those men who wait until middle age before falling in love, and then do it in a big way. (His early escape from the clutches of the designing actress can hardly be called a real love affair.) True, slanderous tongues had striven to undermine his influence by gratuitously providing him with amorous intrigues. One such incident in particular had caused him great distress, reflected by the following letter to Dr. Edmund Gibson, the Bishop of London:

My Lord,
  Some time ago I was informed that your Lordship had received some allegations against me by one   [1] *charging me with committing or offering to commit lewdness with her. I have also been lately informed that your Lordship has been pleased to say, if I solemnly declared my innocence, you should be satisfied. I therefore take this liberty, and do hereby solemnly declare that neither did I ever commit lewdness with her that person, neither did I ever solicit her thereunto, but am innocent in deed, word and thought as touching this thing.*
  As there are other such slanders cast on me, and no less than all manner of evil spoken of me, I must beg leave further to declare mine innocence as to all other women likewise. It is now near twenty years since I began working out my salvation, in all which time God, in

---

[1] A blank is left in the shorthand copy from which we transcribe.

whose presence I speak, has kept me from committing any act of adultery or fornication, or soliciting any person whatsoever thereto. I never did the action, I never spoke a word inducing anyone to such evil, I never harboured any such design in my heart.

If your Lordship requires any further purgation, I am ready to repeat this declaration viva voce, *and to take the blessed Sacrament in proof of it.*

I am, my Lord, your Lordship's dutiful son and servant,
Charles Wesley.

The Foundery,
February 8, 1744/5.

Not only was Charles Wesley guiltless of any gross misbehaviour, but also of the blunders which marred his elder brother's relationships with women. John's cumbersome efforts at love-making eventually drove him for refuge into the arms of a shrew. As for Charles, there seems to have been only the one love affair in his whole life, and it could hardly have turned out better.

It was a case of love at first sight. This is revealed by a chance phrase in a letter of February 1749 to Sally Gwynne:

You have heard me acknowledge that at first sight 'My soul seemed pleased to take acquaintance with thee'. And never have I found such a nearness to any fellow-creature as to you. O that it may bring us nearer and nearer to God, till we are both swallowed up in the immensity of His love!

Happily Charles's journal helps us to fix the date of this first meeting. It was whilst he was staying with the rector of Maesmynis, the Rev. Edward Phillips. On Friday, 28th August 1747, Charles wrote:

Mr. Gwynne came to see me at Mr. Phillips's, with two of his family. My soul seemed pleased to take acquaintance with them.

Sally's companion on that occasion was in all probability her sister Becky, her senior by two years, who was to be her confidante during the courtship and for fifty years after—Becky herself never married. Their younger sister Betty was also initiated into the secret joys and alarms, letters written to one being shared by the others.

Whilst waiting for the return of his brother John from Ireland, Charles accepted Mr. Gwynne's invitation to his home at Garth, where the two brothers held a little conference on the plan of campaign in Dublin. The close friendships which Charles Wesley formed during these few days were followed up by letters from Ireland. The relationship between himself and Sally was supposedly that of spiritual instructor and disciple, Charles being nearly twice her age. He seemed hardly to know how to address her in the first of his letters which has been preserved, so plunged right into it:

Dublin, Sept. 17.

Why did Eternal Wisdom bring us together here, but that we might meet hereafter at His right hand, and sing salvation unto God who sitteth upon the throne, and to the Lamb for ever! Surely the will of God is our sanctification. Even now He waits to be gracious unto you; and before I see you (if ever I see you again upon earth) you will know your Redeemer liveth, and feel His peace and power in your heart. This is my earnest expectation, and my constant prayer. I see you (and so doth my Master) lying on the brink of the pool; and you *have* faith—to be healed. . . . My heart is deeply engaged for you.

When Charles Wesley returned from that first lengthy sojourn in Ireland, it was as a physical wreck. The nursing that he received at Garth from the slender hands of Sally Gwynne and her sisters added a touch of the maternal in her relationship to him. Recovered, and once more an itinerant preacher, he wrote on 28th May 1748:

I cannot forbear a line to my beloved friend, weary as I am with my yesterday's ride of near ninety mile. If the Lord permit, I should rejoice to see you at my return to B[ristol], and so much the rather because I am far from promising myself another safe return from Ireland. . . . But all is dark concerning me, and I struggle in vain to break through into the clear light of eternity.

On 9th August, just before setting sail for Ireland, we find him making a prayer-pact with her:

Remember to meet me always on Monday noon, and every evening at five. Neither would you repent of it if you joined with me constantly in David's resolution, 'At morning, and evening, and *at noon-day*, will I call upon Thee.'

That there was already an 'understanding' between them may be surmised from the emotional undercurrent and lyrical phrases of his letter from Holyhead on 12th August:

Both you and I have still a baptism to be baptized with; and how should we be straitened till it is accomplished! This, this is the one thing needful—not a Friend—not health—not life itself, but the pure perfect love of Christ Jesus. O give me love, or else I die! O give me love, and *let* me die! I am weary of my want of love, weary to death, and would fain throw off this body, that I may love Him who so loved me.
 If you do indeed love me for His sake (and I can as soon doubt of my being alive), O wrestle with that Friend of sinners in my behalf, and let Him not go till He bless me with the sense of His love. How shall I feed His lambs unless I love Him? How shall I give up all, even those Friends who are dearer to me than my own soul? How shall I suffer for One I do not love? O Eternal Spirit of Love, come down into my heart and into my Friend's heart, and knit us together in the bond of perfectness. Lead us by the waters of comfort. Swallow up our will in Thine. Make ready the bride, and then call us up to the marriage supper of the Lamb!

Obviously he had received strict feminine instructions as to taking care of himself, and was resigned to obedience, writing a day later:

My bodily strength is repaired by three days' rest. You will allow me to commend myself. I have not lain on the boards since I left you, and have slept most immoderately till six every morning. This indulgence I impute to [he first wrote 'you', then crossing it out, wrote] *a Friend*, who constantly attends my slumbers, and hovers over me as my Guardian Angel.

You will take advice, I hope, as well as give it, and follow a good example by regular sleeping and rising. You cannot be so exact as me, but do the best you can. Expect to give a strict account of yourself, if we should meet again.

His postscript shows that he had set her on the road to keeping their correspondence safe from prying eyes— 'Don't forget your shorthand.' A month later her maternal influence still continued effective:

I put off my clothes (remembering a Friend's advice) every night, that I may make the most of my strength; and hitherto I feel no weariness by preaching morning and evening to many thousands.

His letter of 17th September included one of those love poems which she was soon to receive quite frequently. Later it was to be published in his *Hymns and Sacred Poems*, altered to disguise its personal origin:

> Two are better far than one,
>   For counsel or for fight!
> How can one be warm alone
>   Or serve his God aright?
> Join we then our hearts and hands;
>   Haste, my sister, dearest friend,
> Run the way of His commands,
>   And keep them to the end! . . .
>
> Who of twain hath made us one,
>   Maintains our unity;
> Jesus is our Corner-stone
>   In whom we both agree;
> Servants of our common Lord,
>   Sweetly of one heart and mind,
> Who can break a threefold cord
>   Or part whom God hath joined?

> Breathes as in us both one soul,
>   When most distinct in place:
> Interposing oceans roll,
>   Nor hinder our embrace:
> Each as on *His* mountain stands,
>   Reach our hearts across the flood,
> Join our hearts, if not our hands,
>   And sing the pard'ning God. . . .

When at last Charles Wesley landed safely at Holyhead on 10th October 1748, he made his way with some difficulty to Garth, where together they 'rejoiced and gave thanks for His innumerable mercies'. For a week he was a welcome guest, preaching meantime in the neighbourhood, and taking the Sunday morning service for the rector at Maesmynis. On this visit he almost certainly discussed the question of marriage with Sally, and his letter to her on 2nd November commenced 'My most beloved Friend'. Two days later he recorded in his journal:

I imparted my design to Mrs. Vigor, [of Bristol] who advised me with all the kindness and freedom of a Christian friend.

There was a bigger hurdle to leap, however. On the 10th he wrote to Sally from London:

I have found my brother well. In much love he salutes you. Tomorrow we devote to [the] conference.

His journal reveals the details of this 'conference':

My brother and I having promised each other, (as soon as he came from Georgia), that we would neither of us marry, or take any step towards it, without the other's knowledge and consent, to-day I fairly and fully communicated every thought of my heart. He had proposed three persons to me, S. P., M. W., and S. G.,[1] and entirely approved my choice of the last. We consulted together about every particular, and were of one heart and mind in all things.

[1] Sally Perrin?, Molly Wells?, and Sally Gwynne.

By the beginning of December he was back again at Garth, wondering how to set about gaining her parents' consent. Eventually Miss Becky broke the news to her mother, who replied that 'she would rather give her child to Mr. Wesley than to any man in England'. Mr. Gwynne was quite content to abide by his wife's decision, which was so far favourable, though the matter was by no means finally settled. On 14th December Charles wrote to Sally:

I rejoice that it depends altogether not on my will, but hers. Her behaviour towards me has obliged me more than my words can express or my life repay. And can I do anything to grieve her generous heart? Not to gain ten thousand worlds; not to gain more—yourself.

In taking such a step, however, Charles dared not depend upon his own judgement, even when confirmed by that of his brother. There followed a round of interviews in which he sought his friends' opinions on the proposed match. The Rev. Vincent Perronet of Shoreham—'the Archbishop of the Methodists', as Charles called him—was one of the first on the list:

I related all which has happened since my parting with my friend and father. He adored the hand of God, visibly appearing in my behalf, cordially joined in the proposal, and encouraged me to depend on God to bring it to pass.

At Lewisham Mrs. Blackwell and Mrs. Dewal

expressed the utmost satisfaction; wondered I should not acknowledge the hand of God *in every step*; assured me they had guessed the person, even the first time they saw her. . . .

One thing was most remarkable, that they were confident the matter when public would be attended with the best consequences, would give general satisfaction to the Church, and even remove many prejudices of the world's.

His letter of 20th December concluded:

Now I must confess that my brother's, Mr. P's, and Mrs. B. and D.'s concurrent judgment has even compelled me to think THIS IS THE LORD'S DOING! THIS IS THE WILL OF GOD CONCERNING ME. They will not allow me to make any doubt of it, but chide me when I express any fear or self-diffidence.

The poems accompanying his letters, however, were still touched with doubt:

> And is there hope for me
> In life's distracting maze?
> And shall I live on earth to see
> A few unruffled days?
> A man of sorrows I,
> A sufferer from the womb,
> 'Twas all my hope in peace to die,
> And rest within my tomb.
>
> How then can I conceive
> A good for me designed,
> The greatest God Himself could give
> The parent of mankind?
> A good by Sovereign Love
> To sinless Adam given,
> His joyous Paradise t'improve,
> And turn his earth to heaven.
>
> God of unbounded grace,
> If yet Thou wilt bestow
> On me the vilest of the race
> Thy choicest gift below;
> My drooping heart prepare
> The blessing to receive,
> And bid the child of sad despair
> With confidence believe. . . .

Other interviews confirmed his awakening confidence. Mrs. Stotesbury at Newington Green, for instance, said:

'The first moment I saw * * I thought in my heart, this is the person *designed* for * *, and I wished it with all my heart.' I asked if my behaviour had given her any ground to think so? 'No,' she answered, 'but the thought sprang up involuntary, irresistible. . . . Since then you both have been laid upon my heart; and all the time you was in Wales I was drawn out in continual prayer for you. . . .'

Nothing I have yet met with has more affected, or *inclined* me to think The Thing is of God.

Charles was so anxious that this proposed marriage should bring no discredit on Methodism that it became a public issue. He wrote from London to Sally on 3rd February 1749:

Through the folly of one, the dotage of another, and the falsehood of a third, this affair is *public enough*, as you observe. But not too public. I will trust Providence for that. My brother supposes that of our society here of two thousand, about eighteen hundred may know of it. Yet to the three opposers above I cannot add a fourth.

Some opposition was encountered, however, caused mainly by jealousy, either vicarious like that of Edward Perronet, who favoured his own sister as Charles Wesley's bride, or open and direct. For both Charles and Sally had rivals. Edward Phillips, the rector of Maesmynis, felt that he had a superior claim to the hand of his beautiful young neighbour, and bombarded her with letters to that effect, even going to the length of intercepting her correspondence. At London, on the other hand, a young lady whom Charles Wesley had baptized in the river at Cowley the previous May, Elizabeth Cart, was heart-sick for him, and Charles wrote to Sally on 27th December 1748:

Our poor dear S. Cart makes my heart ache to see her: she is so above measure dejected. *My* cheerfulness has murdered *hers*. She guesses the cause of my joy, as I do of her sorrow: neither is it in my power to comfort her. You will pity and pray for her, that she faint not in her evil day.

In a month's time, however, he could write:

M[iss] C[art] is more affable, more obliging, more friendly than ever I knew her. She takes the utmost pains to atone for her past behaviour. I receive all in good part, be she sincere, or be she not.

Phillips continued bitter, though his overshadowing presence gradually faded out from their correspondence. For another serious difficulty had not yet been surmounted, that of money.

Charles Wesley had no regular income, yet he had rather light-heartedly promised to provide £100 a year for his bride. The money was not easy to produce, however, so that he set to work to find out what his financial assets really were. On 3rd January 1749 he thus outlined the results of his inquiry to Mrs. Gwynne, as 'Dear Madam':

Till now I neither knew nor cared what my writings and my brother's were worth. But I ordered my printer at B[ristol] to make an exact estimate. His account of their value . . . is £2500, exclusive of the book I am now publishing, which will bring in more than £200 clear, besides a new version of the Psalms worth as much or more, and my journals and sermons, which I am daily called upon to publish. What all these copies amount to I will have computed and sent to you, when you have leisure to examine them.

I am ashamed to trouble you with this strange kind of writing, however necessary. Permit me only to add one thing more. If after the strictest scrutiny you are satisfied as to a provision, and Mr. Gwynne and you see cause to give your consent, I would desire Miss Sally might secure her fortune in case of her own mortality, that it may return to her own family. I seek not hers but her; and if the Lord should give and take away I shall want nothing upon earth. I abhor the thought of being a gainer by her in temporals, and could not rest unless secured from this danger. Your regard for me must not here interpose to hinder what would vindicate my character, and be most for the credit of the Gospel.

In order to ease the financial situation Charles had taken in hand the publication of two volumes of *Hymns and Sacred Poems*—the first such work to be published in his own name and without his brother's supervision. Sally had been asked to prepare for it an index of first lines, and when he sent her the printed leaflet, dated 18th

December 1748, canvassing subscribers, he receipted the attached order form, writing:

> The enclosed shows you my first subscriber: whom I set at the head of my list as a good omen. Many have followed your example already, being readier to part with their money than I to take it.

During all the ups and downs of their tentative engagement, if such it may be called, the two lovers kept the postal services busy. Charles's extant letters for the four months December 1748 to March 1749 would almost fill this book. There was a post out from London every Tuesday, Thursday, and Saturday, and Charles wrote by every available post. Almost as soon as one letter had been despatched another would be started, to be augmented as opportunity offered. Probably the longest was that commenced on Sunday morning, 15th January 1749, after he had received Mrs. Gwynne's comment that she was rather doubtful whether unsold literary works were really sufficient security. He was almost prepared to let the matter end there. Almost, but not quite:

> It is not *fair* for me, in the noon of life, to wish a Friend only in the morning of hers to accompany *me* to Paradise. Your dearest Mother's *consenting so far* is plainly miraculous, and what I never expected, although my friends insisted on it as my duty to make the proposal. I cannot think Providence would suffer the matter to proceed so far, were it to stop here. The hinge on which all turns is not fortune, not even consent of friends, . . . but the glory of God, and the good of souls, (yours especially). If our meeting would really answer those ends I defy all earth and hell to hinder it. If it would not; durst I desire it?

Then he turned to answering in detail her own letters, including references to Phillips and Miss Cart. He told of his visit to Perronet for advice, transcribing a poem deep in pathos which he had composed during his 'dark wet journey to Shoreham'. Next came a journal of

Sunday itself, to be continued on Monday. On Monday evening he answered her letter just received, saying 'I believe God suffers things to continue in suspense for our farther trial', and again discussed the jealousy of Phillips. Extracts from letters of various friends who commended the match were then transcribed, and late on Monday evening he was still writing:

It is late, but I know not how to leave off, my heart so overflows with love toward you. And what shall I say more? All my words and thoughts and life are, under God, devoted to your service. I bless you, and pray Him to bless you, above all that I can ask or think. To His everlasting arms I commit you this night.

The following day his pen was taken up again:

Tuesday.—There is no end of my letter—or of my love, which dictates it. But you will excuse the length, and I hope imitate it. Begin before post-day.

He concluded with a poem of ten verses, commencing:

> Lord, we long to know Thy pleasure,
>   Lift our eyes
>   To the skies,
> Humbly wait Thy leisure . . .

The clouds of uncertainty passed. Mrs. Gwynne saw reason, and John Wesley stood guarantor for the £100 per annum. Charles could hardly believe it when final consent came on January 23rd:

Hope and I had long since shook hands and parted, and all my expectation was to go softly all my days, and be saved at last as by fire. Providence (for I can ascribe it to nothing else) has strangely *brought* me the best gift Heaven could bestow on man in Paradise; at least it *seems*, as it were, within my reach. Yet does my soul *tremble* at the prospect. . . . My every breath *ought* to be prayer or praise. Help me, my beloved Friend, to wrestle for the blessing of Divine love, and now lift up your heart with me in the following words:

> Father of compassions, hear,
> For Jesus' sake alone;
> If we see Thy hand *appear*
> And mark the work *begun,*
> O confirm the sacred sign,
> And all Thine outstretched arm make bare,
> Send us down the gift divine,
> The grace of faith and prayer. . . .

On 5th February he was still calling himself 'a poor unpraying soul', and warning her of his shortcomings:

Your confidence in *me* makes me tremble, lest I should prove a broken reed. For God's sake, and your own, *do not expect too much*! I am a man of like passions—compassed about with infirmities, weak in faith, and wanting in all things. Yet I humbly hope, if God bestows you upon me, He will help me to be helpful, and make all my desires and endeavours for your good *effectual*.

Even on 12th March he still could not feel sure of the event:

If God, whose judgments are a great deep, should at last disappoint me of my hope, what shall I say, or do! My soul shrinks back at the thought, and gives up (with you) all possibility of happiness (instrumental, I mean) on this side eternity. How shall I drag the load of remaining life without you? How can I live out my time with patience? My heart faints and mine eyes overflow at the prospect.—But I *will* hope to be taken from the evil to come, and *first* escape to the land where all things are forgotten.

He went on, however:

Let not your faith be shaken by my weakness and fears. God is all-sufficient. In Christ all fulness dwells. His love alone (was one of us this night caught up to Paradise) could make the survivor happy. And still I hold fast my confidence that we *shall meet* on earth, if it be best. We shall, though parted for a season *first*, to try our faith yet more.

Eventually 8th April came round, and in the little chapel of ease at Llanlleonfel Charles Wesley was united to Sally Gwynne by John Wesley. The event was thus announced to Ebenezer Blackwell:

Garth, April 8, 1749.

MY DEAR FRIEND,

Pray for me. I want your prayers rather than your *congratulations*. Yet I believe God has lent me a great blessing *this day*, and that I *ought* to be thankful, and employ every blessing and every moment to His glory. The following hymn we sang at the altar. You may join with us *now* in singing it:

> Come, thou everlasting Lord,
> By our trembling hearts adored;
> Come, thou heaven-descended Guest,
> Bidden to the marriage-feast.
> Sweetly in the midst appear
> With Thy chosen followers here;
> Grant us the peculiar grace,
> Show to all Thy glorious face. . . .
>
> Stop the hurrying spirits' haste,
> Change the souls' ignoble taste,
> Nature into grace improve,
> Earthly into heavenly love.
> Raise our hearts to things on high,
> To our Bridegroom in the sky,
> Heaven our hope and highest aim,
> Mystic marriage of the Lamb. . . .

CHAPTER VI

FOR BETTER FOR WORSE

On the Easter Sunday prior to his wedding, Charles Wesley had told the congregation at the Foundery, London, that he 'had taken, *not one*, but all of them *for better for worse*, and till death do us part'. He was painfully anxious that marriage should not make him a less effective minister. Hence his careful probing of his friends' opinions. Hence, in part at least, his wavering mind, his fits of depression during the months preceding the 'irrecoverable step'. He was quite determined to be wedded to his work, as well as to his wife.

Modern couples usually start their married life with a journey, and then settle down at home. Charles and Sally Wesley started their married life with a fortnight's honeymoon at her parents' home in Garth—during which time he preached every day—and then he 'cheerfully left [his] partner for the Master's work, and rode on . . . to Bristol', where he promptly fell ill. Recovering a little, he wrote defensively to his brother John:

I was too eager for the work, and therefore believe God checked me by that short sickness. . . . More zeal, more life, more power, I have not felt for some years; (I wish my mentioning this may not lessen it;) so that hitherto marriage has been no hindrance. You will hardly believe it sits so light upon me. I forgot my wife (can you think it?) as soon as I left her. Some farther proof I had of my heart on Saturday last, when the fever threatened most. I did not find, so far as I can say, any unwillingness to die on account of any I should leave behind. Neither did death appear less desirable than formerly; which I own gave me great pleasure, and made me shed tears of joy. I almost believe, nothing shall hurt me; that the world, and the flesh, and the devil, shall keep their distance, or, assaulting, leave me more than conqueror.

He was almost pathetically eager to prove that marriage, far from unfitting him for his spiritual tasks, was a valuable stimulus. On 29th April 1749 he wrote to Ebenezer Blackwell:

A man of business (and consequently hurry) like you can scarce believe me, or I would assure you I have not felt the least hurry or discomposure of mind for some time before and ever since my marriage; which I esteem as a signal favour from God, and a token of good to come.

Less than a week later, though still far from well, he was forcing himself on to his duties in London:

My heart (I own) recoils and trembles. I would impute it to bodily weakness. My too careful friends dissuade me from a journey which they think I am not fit for. Dear M[rs.] V[igor] cried over me last night, till she almost broke my heart. But I must not now begin to favour myself.

That there was still an unspoken doubt lurking in his mind, however, is revealed by his letter to Sally from London on 7th May:

I never remember to have spoken with more life and power. Every word came from my heart, and went to that of all hearers. I cannot be sufficiently thankful for such a blessing, *at such a time*, when I most desired it.

A week later he wrote:

One end of our meeting is evident already—our mutual support and comfort. Never had I a greater appetite for labour, or more life in performing it. . . . We shall both rejoice (I cannot doubt of it) at our union here, throughout all eternity.

In the same letter occurs a touch of sarcasm—or is it *naïveté?*

How is it that my younger female friends, and they only, are afraid my loving you should hinder my loving them? A little time will prove the contrary.

Already he had found in Bristol 'a small, convenient house, £11 a year, next Mrs. Vigor's', but Mrs. Gwynne wanted them to delay setting up house for some months or possibly years. This at first seems to have fitted in nicely with Charles's views, for he wrote to his brother, 'You, I think, will not hinder our living as pilgrims'. On 7th May, however, he announced that he had secured in London a suitable servant for 'when we take a house'—having erased the 'if' with which he had originally commenced the phrase. A few days later he suggested their setting up house after a month or two at Ludlow, whither the Gwynne family were removing, and on 27th May, his preaching tour to London over, the house in Charles Street, Bristol, was finally rented. At the beginning of June he rejoined Sally at Ludlow, and then took her on a tour of the societies, a great welcome meeting her everywhere. They returned to Ludlow in time for John Wesley's visit on 10th August, when John's signature was appended to the document settling £100 a year on Charles as his share in the profits from their joint publications.

Returning from Ireland with John Wesley was Grace Murray, already in a manner betrothed to him, though this was apparently kept secret. Charles travelled with his brother and Grace to London, his thought and speech revolving all the time around his Sally. The great spiritual blessings which his marriage had already brought, and its promise for the future, would blind his eyes to the fact that his two companions were themselves warming to the subject. He returned to Bristol all unconscious of having added fuel to the fire. For although marriage in his own case certainly seemed likely to be a spiritual aid and a blessing to the Methodist cause, for his brother it was different. For him marriage was unthinkable. It would certainly be a dereliction of duty, for the main burden of leadership, which entailed constant itinerancy,

WESLEY						71

rested inevitably on John's shoulders. When in December 1748 George Whitefield had urged that both the Wesley brothers should marry, Charles had 'pleaded hard for [his] brother's exemption'.

Charles and Sally Wesley set up house in Charles Street, Bristol, on 1st September 1749, rather dreading the expected stream of visitors:

How the great world and we shall agree, I cannot say, but shall see by and by. If they pour in upon us so as quite to swallow up our time, I shall run away outright, to London, Cornwall, Newcastle, Ireland, or America.

So he wrote to Ebenezer Blackwell on 4th September, and showed the spirit in which he approached his new venture by quoting 'part of [his] *first* family hymn':

> God of faithful Abraham, hear
>   His feeble son and Thine;
> In Thy glorious power appear,
>   And bless my just design.
> Lo! I come to serve Thy will,
>   All Thy blessed will to prove,
> Fired with patriarchal zeal,
>   And pure primeval love.
>
> Me and mine I fain would give
>   A sacrifice to Thee,
> By the ancient model live,
>   The true simplicity;
> Walk as in my Maker's sight,
>   Free from worldly guile and care,
> Praise my innocent delight,
>   And all my business prayer. . . .

The Wesleys' first month of married life in their own home at Bristol was rudely shattered by one of the strangest matrimonial entanglements in history, in which the main actors were John Wesley, his trusted preacher John Bennet, Grace Murray, and Charles Wesley himself. All four have in turn been blamed for what was almost certainly a bewildering mixture of misunderstandings, all of which have not yet been resolved. Both John Wesley and John Bennet believed themselves engaged to Grace Murray, who did not clearly know where she stood, but was eventually swept off her feet and into the arms of Bennet by the impetuous Charles. That Charles Wesley planned to outwit his brother seems certain; that he did so from the worthiest of motives even more certain. The thought of his brother's marrying at all was bad enough. But from the evidence which he possessed at the time it seemed that John Wesley was not only in danger of 'marrying beneath him' but—a much more serious matter—of bringing scandal on his own good name and that of the Church. Charles visualized himself in the role of a *deus ex machina*, charged with the duty of saving John Wesley in spite of himself. He acted hastily, passionately, but as the loyal servant of God. His attitude is revealed in a letter to Grace Murray:

Fain would I hope that you can say something in your defence (when I come to talk with you) which now I know not. But the case appears thus to me:

You promised J[ohn] B[ennet] to marry him—since which you engaged yourself to another.

How is this possible? And who is that other? One of such importance that his doing so dishonest an action would destroy both himself and me and the whole work of God. It was on the very brink of ruin; but the snare is broken, and we are delivered.

Wildly he dashed about: from Bristol to Leeds, from Leeds to Newcastle; across country to Whitehaven after his brother; and back again to the Dales and Newcastle. With Grace Murray safely married to John Bennet on 3rd October, he could at last breathe a sigh of relief, and return with an easy conscience to Bristol, preaching as he went.

The fact that he had conscientiously acted for the best did not prevent a dangerous breach with his stricken brother. A peacemaker was on the scene, however, in the person of their former comrade George Whitefield, who helped greatly in the partial clearing up of this tragedy of errors. Something of Charles's own efforts to heal the wound may be seen from his letters to Bennet, letters in which John Wesley is thinly disguised as 'our friend', for far too many letters had already gone astray. On 8th January 1750 he wrote:

What provoked our friend to that rash exposing *himself* (not you, or me) was my showing *my* account to some of the preachers. Thence the Enemy took occasion, and urged him to read his to our stewards and a few more. But it is over now, and all is quiet.

Our Enemy's design is to induce him or you or me to *publish* that affair, by any means; so to stop the course of the gospel, and scatter the flock. Let us not be ignorant of his devices. All private resentment *must* be sacrificed to public good. . . . For God's sake, and His people's, possess your soul in patience. I have a need of patience too. It is a sifting time: yet the Lord waits to be gracious, and gives great testimony to the word of His grace. And there is a wonderful revival of the work in London. God forbid we should obstruct, much less destroy it. But this would be the sure effect of our vindicating ourselves. Let us leave it all to Him, against hope believing in hope, and standing still to see His salvation. . . .

Our friend and I have agreed to bury all in oblivion; which you will be glad to hear, for his sake.

I hope my last did not miscarry, wherein I advised your partner never never more to write to or even to wish to converse with ——.

The ashes were still smouldering, however, and care was needed to prevent their being fanned into a flame. On 2nd March he wrote again to Bennet:

He is *not* for printing, nor ever was. There your correspondent abuses your credulity: and I cannot excuse him, whoever he be, of rashness, and the *appearance* at least of mischief-making. Be on your guard against such.

I have talked with our friend at Oxford, and find him quite willing to bury all past matters in oblivion. This is surely most agreeable to the will of God. God has blessed his labours of late more than ever.

Therefore *we* ought to bear, and wait, till the cock crow. I suffer all things that the gospel be not hindered.

On 22nd August 1750 Grace Bennet gave birth to her first baby boy, named John after his father. About this time there seems to have been some interview, or possibly letter, between her and John Wesley. Charles laboured hard to prevent any further risk of stirring up memories, writing to Bennet on 3rd September:

You must pass an Act of Eternal Oblivion on all sides: but take care not to bring our two friends together again! It was an amazing oversight both in Grace and you, and looked like infatuation. If you regard me as your real friend (and I know you do), follow my Christian advice, and never let them meet till they meet among the sheep on the right hand. I can easily convince you, if it be not self-evident, of the necessity of this advice.

On 15th December he reverted to the subject:

If the Lord Himself had not been on our side, well may we both and all Israel say, 'They had swallowed us up quick, and *by us ourselves* destroyed the whole work of God.' . . . It is all over with our friend. Only me he cannot love as before. But I must have patience and suffer all things that the gospel be not hindered.

Charles was right in believing that relations between himself and his brother would never be quite the same again. It was soon to be proved. Less than sixteen months after Grace Murray had been snatched from his grasp, John Wesley made another matrimonial venture. In accordance with their pact he informed Charles, who wrote in his journal for 2nd February 1751:

I was thunderstruck, and could only answer, he had given me the first blow, and his marriage would come like the *coup de grace*. . . . Groaned all day, and several following ones under my own and the people's burden. I could eat no pleasant food, nor preach, nor rest, either by night or by day.

Although he had observed their agreement thus far, by informing Charles of his intentions, John Wesley was not going to risk any more interference. A fortnight later, having satisfied himself that his prospective wife would not attempt to hinder his work for Methodism, he married the well-to-do widow of Anthony Vazeille, his brother not hearing about the event till some days later.

Again Charles Wesley was up in arms. And again his main fear was of the unhappy repercussions which his brother's marriage would probably have on the Methodist societies. As far as the unsuitability of the match was concerned, he was on this occasion most certainly right. Another letter to Bennet, written on 15th March 1751, reflects his grief and anxiety:

You and your partner must make me amends for the loss of my brother, . . . whose love I have small hopes of recovering in this world. But I find my heart knit still closer to you, and am humbly confident that neither life nor death shall be able to separate us.

In a former letter I *said* what I *thought*; and upon reasonable proof. Long since then my brother fell in the way of his present wife. 'Happy is the Wooing, not long in Doing' says the proverb, which he seems willing to verify. I labour with all my power to quiet the people, and (blessed be God!) my labour is not in vain.

That Charles Wesley did honestly strive to ensure that the success of this hasty marriage should not be prejudiced by his own attitude seems to be proved by the following extracts from his journal:

Wed. Feb. 27. My brother came to the chapel-house with his wife. I was glad to see him; saluted her; stayed to hear him preach; *but ran away when he began his apology.*

Thurs. March 14. *Saw the necessity of reconciliation with my brother, and resolved to save the trouble of umpires.*[1]

Fri. March 15. Called on my sister; kissed and assured her I was perfectly reconciled to her and to my brother.

[1] Transcribed from the shorthand. See note, p. 6.

Tues. March 19. Brought my wife and sister together, and took all opportunities of showing the latter my sincere respect and love.

Mrs. John Wesley was her own worst enemy, however. Twenty years later her long-suffering husband dealt dispassionately with the accusations which she complained had been levelled against her:

You say you are accused . . . 'of being a Vixen'. I do not well understand the term. But if it means a woman of an uneasy temper, and bitter of speech, I cannot deny it. For fifty years I have had much commerce with mankind: but of all whom I have conversed with, another of so unhappy a temper and so provoking a tongue I have not known.

Within a few months of their marriage this evil temper had betrayed itself in jealousy over John Wesley's relationships with the women in his societies. Charles Wesley endeavoured in vain to heal the breach. Mrs. John Wesley was not an easy woman to handle. And she believed that she had cause for grievance against Charles himself. Indeed, in the letter quoted above John Wesley had suggested:

The first object of your jealousy, I believe, was my brother; you was extremely jealous of my trusting him more than you.

Another thorn in her flesh was Charles Wesley's marriage settlement, which John thus defended:

I settled upon my brother and his heirs an hundred pounds a year out of the money arising from the sale of books (about two hundred pounds a year). But observe. It was no more than his due. For so much comes from the sale of his hymns.

All things considered, it is not surprising that Charles Wesley's genuine attempts to pacify his sister-in-law were not eminently successful. After a time even Edward Perronet, who appears to have played some part in bringing Mrs. Vazeille and John Wesley together, began to despair of the situation, so that in September 1753 Charles wrote to his wife:

I met N. Perronet and had much pertinent talk with him. He has utterly disobliged a FRIEND of ours by assuring her I was not her enemy; and gives her up as absolutely untractable.

John Wesley's serious illness a month or two later seemed likely to bring about a reconciliation. Charles wrote:

My brother entreated me yesterday, and his wife, to forget all that is past, on both sides. I *sincerely* told him I would for his, as well as Christ's sake. My sister said the same.

Much to his own surprise, as well as that of others, John Wesley arose from his supposed death-bed. And the armed neutrality continued.

Henceforth Mrs. John Wesley usually appeared in Charles Wesley's letters to his wife under the euphemism of 'my best friend'. On 29th April 1755 he wrote from Leeds:

I am going to breakfast with Miss Norton, who is as far from the spirit of my *Best Friend*, as East is from West. What shall you and I do to love her better? 'Love your enemies' is with men impossible: but is anything too hard for God? I fear you do not *constantly* pray for her. I *must* pray, or sink—into the spirit of revenge.

In 1758 he wrote:

You 'fear an intimacy' with my *Best Friend*. (Such I must always acknowledge her.) But I will trust you for that. What communication hath light with darkness?

In 1766 he warned Sally:

My brother and sister will call on you, I presume, next Wednesday. She continues quite placid and tame. You can be courteous, without trusting her.

Even as late as 1780 he could write, 'Henceforth, a Friend and I shall only meet like two buckets in a well'.

It was with real knowledge of the hazards that on 30th August 1782 Charles Wesley penned some thoughts on marriage for his son:

DEAR CHARLES,
If any man would learn to pray (the proverb says) let him go to sea. I say, if any man would learn to pray, let him think of marrying. . . . No one step or action in life has so much influence on eternity as marriage. It is an heaven or an hell (they say) in this world: much more so in the next.

By that time his 'best friend' lay in her grave, so that he refrained from using the obvious illustration of the dangers of an over-hasty match. Perhaps he realized also, to use George Whitefield's phrase, that after all his brother's marriage had been 'overruled for good'. It had certainly warded off any temptation to settle down. As Charles had written to his wife in 1759, after tracing a slander against himself to 'the root of bitterness, *my best friend*': 'I do not wonder that my poor brother trembles and quakes at the thought of coming to London.' The ties of family responsibility, the allurements of domesticity, meant nothing to John Wesley. The world continued still to be his parish. Charles did not so easily escape the dreaded snares of matrimony.

CHAPTER VII

PURGING THE PREACHERS

METHODISM had quickly taken firm hold in London and Bristol, and between these two centres John and Charles Wesley were constantly travelling, building up loyal bands of local helpers who appear frequently in Charles's letters, employing also more and more lay preachers to assist during their absences. For other places were clamouring for attention—Ireland, Cornwall, the Midlands, and the North, where Newcastle was the third point for the Methodist triangulation of England. From all sides arose the outcry for more preachers, more visits from one or other of the Wesley brothers.

Here was John Bennet, for instance, complaining that since his marriage to Grace Murray the Wesleys had neglected his 'round' in Derbyshire, Staffordshire, Cheshire, and Lancashire. Tactfully Charles endeavoured to pacify him, writing on 1st May 1750:

The uncertainty of my brother's motions keeps me in suspense. If he makes any stay in Ireland, I must hover between Bristol and London meanwhile. Probably in a month's time I shall guess whenabouts I may begin my journey northward.

'Whether we have very much neglected your part of the vineyard *designedly*, God knows'—that is sure; and *you* know that we have but one body apiece, which can be in but one place at a time. Whether you might not have had an exhorter more frequently spared you, I cannot say, not being the orderer of their motions: but I believe my brother makes the most of them, and disposes of them more wisely than I or you could do. The very reason, I presume, why he leaves your parts so much to yourself is his just opinion of your diligence and fidelity. However, be not discouraged. The Lord of the harvest shall in His own time send you more fellow-labourers. Till then, do all you can, whether more or less, and your labour will not be in vain.

Two months later he was still staving off criticism:

My brother's long and dangerous stay in Ireland has confined me to London and Bristol. It may be a month still before he returns. Then perhaps I may begin my journey to the north.

With a sigh of relief he wrote on 10th August:

My brother is come to Bristol, and gone immediately to Cornwall. At his return we shall one of us hasten to the north.

At last on 3rd September he could report: 'On Monday sennight my brother sets out from London for the north.' The plan was altered, however, perhaps to avoid those complications with Grace Bennet which Charles Wesley dreaded. Charles set off instead. Near Islington his mare threw him, then fell upon him. This accident, with the addition of a painful boil, involved the postponing of his journey. The north must wait. The following February John Wesley planned to go, but a fall on the ice delayed *his* journey—though it apparently hastened his marriage to Mrs. Vazeille. Towards the end of March 1751 John finally made the long-delayed visit to the north, though it had to be rather a hurried one. Such were some of the difficulties of maintaining oversight of the ever-increasing Methodist societies.

At the end of June 1751 Charles Wesley also set out for the north, to tie up the loose ends unavoidably left by his brother, and also to recruit the sorely needed travelling preachers who should take much of this burden off their shoulders. The previous September John had given Charles written instructions about his travelling duties:

I wish you could talk a little with every preacher and every exhorter that comes in your way. Perhaps you may find some who are capable of being taken into the general work.

Another urgent need had arisen in the meantime, however, that of inquiring strictly into the suitability of the preachers already employed. It was perhaps inevitable that in these early years a few unstable or unworthy men should have crept into the ranks of Wesley's helpers. One of their number, James Wheatley, had brought Methodism into bad odour by his amatory adventures. The two brothers had written a joint letter of suspension, and Charles had recorded in his journal:

It put my brother and me upon a resolution of strictly examining into the life and moral behaviour of every preacher in connexion with us; and the office fell upon me.

In spite of Charles's somewhat impetuous nature, John felt secure in entrusting him with this difficult and responsible task. He had already shown himself greatly concerned about the character and abilities of the preachers, and had played a subsidiary part in their stationing. One of his shortest letters had been written early in 1746 to that valiant stonemason of Birstall, John Nelson, then stationed in Bristol:

MY BROTHER,
You must watch and pray, labour and suffer. My spirit is with you. You will shortly be wanted in Yorkshire.
                                                             Farewell.

His concern for the preachers' welfare is also shown in his letters to Joseph Cownley, commencing in 1749, when Cownley was stationed in Ireland. On 9th April of that year, for instance, he had written:

MY DEAR BROTHER,
'Tis not possible for us to judge of your differences, till my brother sees and hears you all together. His coming, I doubt not, will compose all. You was backward in writing. Mend in this also. I hope your soul begins to subside. Watch and pray, that you enter not further into temptation. . . . The Lord bless you, and keep you from all pride and self-seeking.
                                                             Farewell.

Charles Wesley was not opposed to lay preaching as such. In March 1740 he had taken Thomas Maxfield with him on a preaching tour, and had suggested to William Seward that he too should begin to expound—though in September of that year he reported unfavourably on Seward's Calvinistic preaching:

I . . . heard him with pain. It was not so bad as I feared, nor so good as to make me believe him called to the work.

(A month later William Seward was killed whilst preaching, the first Methodist martyr.) Although quite ready to acknowledge the value of the noble lay preachers of Methodism, however, Charles Wesley was certainly not prepared to give them *carte blanche*. They must be kept under strict supervision. When he was touring Cornwall in 1746, for instance, he had written to his brother:

Both shepherds and sheep had been scattered in the late cloudy day of persecution; but the Lord gathered them again and kept them together by means of some of the brethren who began to exhort their companions, some one or more in every society. No less than four of them sprang up in Gwennap. I talked closely with each this morning, and found no reason to doubt of their having been used by God *thus far*: advised, and charged them not to stretch themselves beyond their measure by speaking *out* of the society, or fancying themselves ministers or public teachers. If they keep within their bounds, as they promise and I believe, they will be useful in the Church: and I would to God all the Lord's people were such prophets as these!

So it was that in 1751 John Wesley entrusted to his brother the vital task of touring England with the specific purpose of 'purging the preachers', of inquiring into their qualifications for the work and dismissing those who were unsatisfactory. Charles kept careful journals of his activities, which he sent periodically in lengthy letters to John. From Leeds he wrote, in shorthand:

I see every day the wisdom of not limiting myself. Here is such an open door as compels me to stay; and my chief design for coming seems likely to succeed. Mich. Fenwick is here. I keep him with me, that I may fully prove him. I shall do nothing rashly, and believe nothing without full proof. Three more women I have found out, whom the shepherd [i.e. James Wheatley] *has wellnigh devoured—rather I should call him a wolf in sheep's clothing.*

John urged his brother to move cautiously, for fear that they should be left with even fewer preachers. He advised leniency where a preacher was incompetent, though not immoral, saying 'We must have a supply; and of the two, I prefer grace before gifts'. To which Charles replied:

Are not both indispensably necessary? Has not the cause suffered, in Ireland especially, through the insufficiency of the preachers? Should we not first regulate, reform, and bring into discipline the preachers we have, before we look for more?

Whilst he was at Leeds, Charles fell dangerously ill with a fever. On Sunday, 28th July, he wrote:

I rose at eight, but was forced to bed again by ten. A shivering fit shook me most violently for two hours, but did not prevent my dictating to S[arah] Perrin, who wrote my confused thoughts concerning the state of the Church. To me they seemed material, if to none else; and I could not deliver my own soul unless I left them behind me.

These 'confused thoughts' were apparently enshrined in a long letter to his friend Lady Huntingdon, which went astray and came into his brother's hands. As a candid (though maybe incorrect) diagnosis of the growing pains from which Methodism was suffering, it should be quoted at some length:[1]

I must leave you my mind in few words. Unless a sudden remedy be found, the preachers will destroy the work of God.

---

[1] The very faulty spelling of this dictated letter is corrected. Although headed 'Leeds Agust ye 4. 1752' there is little doubt that the date should really be 1751. The letter opened by announcing that his earlier attempt to summarize the position had had to be abandoned because of his illness.

What has wellnigh ruined many of them is their being taken from their trades. . . . The tinner, barber, thatcher, forgot himself, and set up for a gentleman, and looked out for a fortune, having lost the only way of maintaining himself. Some have been betrayed by pride into still greater sins, and are (unless stopped in time) to do the Devil far more service than ever they did God. Some have fallen into grievous crimes and must therefore be put away. What will then become of them? Will they not cause the same confusion that is now in Wales? Will not each set up for himself, and make a new party, sect, or religion? Or supposing we have authority enough to quash them while we live, or while my brother and I live, who can stop them after our death? It does not satisfy my conscience to say, God look to that. We must look to that now ourselves, or we tempt God. . . .

The only effectual way in my judgement is to set them to work again, to prove them heartily which has any grace left, and which has not; who is sent of God, and who of flesh and blood, sloth, pride, and the Devil. . . . The man who consents to labour at times at his calling proves his obedience and humility both to us and the Church; he stops the mouths of gainsayers; relieves the poor people of that intolerable burden; and if God withdraws His gifts, he is but where he was before. If God continues to use him . . . his trade [leaves] him no vacant time for sauntering, gossiping, and courting; and if he is inclined to marry, the Church is spared from being burdened with his wife and children.

My proposal then is this:

First, that every preacher that has a trade return to it (except a very few who cannot); that he labours with his hands like Paul Greenwood [or] T. Westall by day, and preach mornings &c [*sic*], tarrying at his own place of abode and the neighbouring towns; that now and then he be permitted to make an excursion, or perhaps take a journey to distant societies, and then return to his trade again.

Secondly, that no future preacher be ever taken from his business or once permitted to preach, till the point is set how he is to be maintained.

Thirdly, that no one be allowed to preach with us, till my brother and I have heard him with our own ears, and talked fully with him, and if needs [be] to keep him with us some days.

These are some of my first rude thoughts on the occasion.

The closing part of this letter ventured on even more dangerous ground:

The second reason which I have for insisting on the labourers keeping themselves (which I cannot mention to my brother lest it should be a reason with him against it) is, namely, [that] it will break his power, their not depending on him for bread, and reduce his authority within due bounds, as well as guard against that rashness and credulity of his, which has kept me in continual awe and bondage for many years. Therefore I shall insist on their working as the one point, the single condition, of my acting in concert with him. Because without this I can neither trust them nor him. If he refuses I will give both preachers and society to his sole management, for this ruin shall not be under my hands. If he complies, I hope to take up my cross and bear it more cheerfully than ever I have done heretofore.

As might be expected, when this letter strayed into John Wesley's hands it evoked some sharp words of rebuke. Nevertheless, a compromise was eventually reached which enabled Charles to continue in partnership with his brother.

Having unburdened himself to Lady Huntingdon, and having recovered his strength a little, Charles continued with his investigations. On 5th August he wrote from Leeds to his brother:

Went to the Room that I might hear with my own ears one of whom many strange things had been told me.[1] I attended diligently in a little room adjoining. But such a preacher have I never heard, and hope I never shall again! It was beyond all description! I can't say he preached false doctrine, or true, or any doctrine at all, but pure unmixed nonsense. Not one sentence did he utter that could do the least good (to?) any one soul. Now and then a text of Scripture or a verse-quotation was dragged in by (the?) head and shoulders. I could scarce refrain from stopping him. . . . He set my blood a-galloping, and threw me into such a sweat that I expected the fever to follow. . . . Of this I am infallibly sure, that if ever he had a gift for preaching, he has now *totally* lost it.

[1] Michael Fenwick.

A week later he was at Newcastle, writing to John Bennet:

Your last helped on the work of God for which He has sent me into His vineyard at this time: and it supplied me with more abundant proof of R. G.'s utter unworthiness to preach the Gospel. I have accordingly stopped him, and shall tomorrow send him back to his proper business. A friend of ours (without God's counsel) made a preacher of a tailor. I, with God's help, shall make a tailor of him again.

You will not (I am persuaded) rejoice in evil, but in evil prevented and good secured by this thing. And pray earnestly for me, that the Lord may guide and direct me in my *most important* concern—to purge the Church, beginning with the labourers.

For this end, I say again in God's name, come and help me. On (the?) 6th of September I trust to see Leeds: on Wednesday, September 11th to meet in conference as many of the preachers as can be got together. Bring you all you can; and give notice everywhere I have silenced another scandalous preacher, and sent a third back to his trade.

One of the preachers was narrowly reprieved in response to the pleadings of the Rev. William Grimshaw, who gathered with the others for the conference at Leeds. Charles wrote from Grimshaw's wife's home:

Ewood, Sept. 16.

DEAR B[ROTHER] SHENT,

I leave this word of notice with you for our sons in the Gospel, (as?) Assistants or Preachers in any degree.

At the desire of a very dear and faithful brother, I have consented to let W[illiam] D[arney] preach among our children as *heretofore*, although I believe his spirit is still whole and unbroken. But on these conditions I consent:

1. That he does not rail, or speak against anyone, much less any labourer.
2. That he does not beg off our people.
3. That he does not print any more of his nonsense, and
4. That he does not introduce the use of his doggerel hymns in any of our societies. I cannot in conscience agree to his putting nonsense into their mouths. Indeed they themselves would never consent to it. But he has utterly refused to promise forbearance: therefore I have promised him that in

whatsoever society of ours he uses his own verses, in that society *he shall preach no more.*
                    Witness my hand.   C. W.

John Bennet had attended this Leeds conference in 1751, but his own already suspicious mind was soon being influenced by two of the disaffected preachers whom Charles Wesley had dismissed, and who immediately started circulating slanders about him. There seems to have been a possibility that the Rev. William Grimshaw himself might be estranged. After striving all he could to prevent Bennet's leaving the Methodists, Charles wrote sadly to him on 18th May 1752:

MY DEAR BROTHER,
    . . . I am told that you have spoke[n] much evil of me, upon Trathen's and Web's testimony: but I cannot, will not believe it, till I have *your* own answer, if these things are so?
    'Many heavy things' (you write) 'have been laid both to my charge and my brother's, and other preachers now labouring with us.'
    I know NO ONE of our preachers NOW who can be *justly* charged with sin: if you or any man does, I shall thank you for informing me of the fact. Without *proof* I ought not to receive an accusation against any of them.
    My brother stands or falls to his own Master.
    If either Trathen or Web spoke those vile things of me (which I have lately heard of) while I was in the county, and you did not apprise me of them, I should ask, Is this thy kindness to thy friend? Is this thy justice? Is it doing as you would be done by, or as I have acted towards you? I never have, and trust I never shall, believe evil of you, or any testimony whatsoever, till I have given you an opportunity of answering for yourself.
    Till I know all the particulars, I can only give a general answer. And I do utterly deny all which I have hitherto heard laid to my charge by your two foul-mouthed informers. *Friends* you would not call them, if you knew them. . . .
    I am (and cannot help being)
            Your faithful, but afflicted, friend,
    Bristol.   .   C. Wesley.
        May 18.

To the end of his days Charles Wesley continued anxious to improve the standard of Methodist preaching, even though he was somewhat caustic at times in his expressions of disapproval. In a shorthand addition to a journal sent to his brother in October 1756, he gave his impressions of a Scottish preacher stationed in Yorkshire:

Alex. Coats is *come. He may have both sense and grace: but I wish he had a little more utterance. I am of George Whitefield's mind, that he will never do for Leeds. He is a barbarian to me, I am sure, for I can't understand one word in three which he speaks.*

In December 1772 he wrote from Bristol about one of the most famous of his brother's lay preachers, that pioneer of American Methodism who would preach with his drawn sword laid across the open Bible, Captain Thomas Webb—though again his remarks were carefully shrouded in shorthand:

Your captain has done much good: because God sends by whom He will. He is a strange man, and very much of an enthusiast. Cannot you persuade him to keep his abundance of visions and revelations to himself? At least not to publish them indifferently to all. I have heard him myself. He has much life and zeal, though far from being a clear or good preacher. I believe you may depend upon his account of America.

Writing to Joseph Benson a few months later, he described Captain Webb as 'an inexperienced, honest, zealous, loving enthusiast'.

Comparatively few of Charles Wesley's letters to the itinerant preachers of Methodism appear to have survived. There is evidence that he kept regularly in touch with a number of them by correspondence, even during his later years, when the shadow of misunderstanding had crept between them. To Joseph Bradford, reporting from Ireland John Wesley's serious illness and expected death, he replied:

Bristol, June 29, 1775.
DEAR JOSEPH,
  Be of good cheer: the Lord liveth; and all live to Him.
  Your last is just arrived; and cuts off all hope of my brother's recovery. . . . The people here, and in London, and every place, are swallowed up in sorrow: but sorrow and death will soon be swallowed up in life everlasting.
  You will be careful of my brother's papers, etc., till you see his executors. God shall reward your fidelity and love. . . .
  Yours of the 20th I have this moment received. It only confirms my fears. My brother (soon after you wrote) in all probability entered into the joy of his Lord. Yet write again, and send the particulars. I have not (and never more shall have) strength for such a journey. The Lord prepare us for a speedy removal to our heavenly country!

In the same year he wrote to Thomas Rankin in America, where the lot of the Methodist preacher was anything but simple:

March 1, 1775.
MY DEAR BROTHER,
  To spare you the expense, I delayed answering your letter; but I bear you always on my heart, and rejoice when the Lord blesses you with success. . . .
  As to the public affairs, I wish you to be like-minded with me. I am of neither side, and yet of both: on the side of New England, and of Old. Private Christians are excused, exempted, privileged, to take no part in civil troubles. We love all, and pray for all, with a sincere and impartial love. Faults there may be on both sides; but such as neither you nor I can remedy.

One of the last letters he wrote, on 13th January 1788, was a friendly note to Samuel Bradburn, the 'Methodist Demosthenes' who visited him on his death-bed and preached his funeral sermon, describing him to a friend as 'a great Divine, without the least contempt for the meanest of his brethren'. Charles's letter consisted largely of requests to be kept in touch with the news of Methodist preachers and their wives, though he was resigned to the fact that he himself was out of the main stream of events:

DEAR SAM,

Send, if you cannot bring me word, how your Sophia fares? Whether Mrs. Brittle[1] is brought to bed, and of what? How he does? How the Governor, and J. Atlay, and Sam Tooth.

I am become as a dead man out of mind, and am content.

Send me the history of your Covenant night. I would gladly join you in renewing the Covenant at West Street. . . .

What day does my B(rother set ou?)t for Bristol? or where? When the Dr.? [Coke].

Adieu.

Although even the preachers who differed from Charles Wesley realized his sterling sincerity, his self-effacing humility, a measure of estrangement came about between them. The cause was not any deficiency in the morals or abilities of a few preachers, but the tendency of a growing number to favour a breach with the Church of England.

[1] Probably the wife of Jeremiah Brettell.

CHAPTER VIII

THE OLD SHIP

EVEN before the first Methodist Conference had been held Charles Wesley had warned his elder brother against the danger of the Methodists deserting 'the old ship', as they both called the mother Church. On 5th March 1744, under the impending shadow of war and civil disturbances, John Wesley had written a loyal address to the King. The following day Charles remonstrated with him by letter:

My objection to your address in the name of the Methodists is, that it would constitute us a sect; at least it would *seem to allow* that we are a body distinct from the national Church, whereas we are only a sound part of that Church. Guard against this.

Henceforth Charles Wesley believed that one of his main tasks was to prevent his brother, and more especially the lay preachers, from discarding their allegiance to the Established Church. His 1751 inquiry into the character of the Methodist preachers was followed by written bonds of agreement between the Wesley brothers and the preachers, one document drawn up by Charles himself on 16th March 1752 binding the signatories 'never to leave the communion of the Church of England without the consent of all whose names are subjoined'.

For a year or two things went fairly smoothly. Then the subdued impatience of those preachers who in self-defence had had to license themselves as Protestant Dissenters began to reveal itself openly, and even John Wesley wondered whether after all he was making a mistake in keeping up his appearance of loyalty. Toward the end of 1754 the pattern which was to be aimed at for thirty years made itself clear—administration of the Sacraments by Methodist preachers, who might even be ordained by John Wesley, yet all without any avowed separation from the Church of England. Charles Wesley wrote in his shorthand diary:

Oct. 17. Sister Macdonald first, and then sister Clay, informed me that Charles Perronet[1] gave the Sacrament to the preachers Walsh and Deaves, and then to twelve at sister Garder's, in the Minories. . . .

Oct. 19. I was with my brother, who said nothing of Perronet except 'We have in effect ordained already.' He urged me to sign the preachers' certificates: was inclined to lay on hands, and to let the preachers administer. . . .

October 24. Was with my brother. He is wavering: but willing to wait before he ordains or separates.

A few weeks later we find him trying to muster some defenders to the cause of the Church of England. He wrote to the Rev. Walter Sellon, formerly a Methodist preacher and a master at Kingswood School:

I have seen your honest friendly letter to C[harles] P[erronet], for which I thank you both in behalf of myself and the Church of England.

You see through him and his fellows. Pride, cursed pride, has perverted him and them, and unless the Lord interposes will destroy the work of God, and scatter us all as sheep upon the mountains.

In your fidelity to my old honoured Mother you are a man after my own heart. I always loved you, but never so much as now. . . . How unlike the spirit of poor Perronet and his associates! What a pity such spirits should have any influence over my brother! They are continually urging him to a separation. That is, to pull down all he has built, to put a sword in our enemies' hands, to destroy the work, scatter the flock, disgrace himself, and go out—like the snuff of a candle.

May I not desire it of you as a debt you owe the Methodists and me, and the Church, as well as him, to write him a full, close, plain transcript of your heart on the occasion? . . .

[1] Son of the Vicar of Shoreham.

I stand alone, as our preachers imagine. Nevertheless the Lord stands by me. Fain would they thrust me out, that they may carry all before them.

On 14th December he pleaded with Sellon once more:

Write again, and spare not. My brother took no notice to me of your letter. Since the Melchisedechians have been taken in, I have been excluded [from] his Cabinet Council. They know me too well to trust him with me. He is come so far as to believe a separation quite lawful, only not yet expedient. They are indefatigable in urging him to go so far that he may not be able to retreat. He may *lay on hands*, say they, without separating. I charge you keep it to yourself *that I stand in doubt of him*: which I tell you that you may pray for him the more earnestly, and write to him the more plainly.

Sellon's letters had their effect, and in February 1755 Charles could write more cheerfully about his brother:

He has spoken as strongly of late in behalf of the Church of England as I could wish; and everywhere declares he never intends to leave her.

The following Conference dealt at length with the question of separation, and Charles wrote home to his wife:

I left the brethren in conference—but had quite enough of them first. Yet I don't repent my trouble. . . . All agreed not to separate. So the wound is healed—slightly.

'Slightly.' He still feared for the future, and took the precaution of compiling a list of those preachers present at the Conference who favoured administering the Sacraments. The postscript to his letter, written from Rotherham, shows that he was determined to take active steps to safeguard the Church:

I have delivered my own soul in this society, and exhorted them to continue stedfast in fellowship with the Church of England. The same exhortation I hope to leave with every society throughout the land. On such an occasion you will cheerfully spare me.

Toward the end of May he struck a new blow for the Church, reporting to his wife from London:

> On Thursday I read my Epistle a second time, to a crowded audience, and yesterday at the watch-night. Seven hundred are sent by this day's carrier.

The reference was to one of his most important letters, though this time a letter in verse, the first such to be published, entitled *An Epistle to the Reverend Mr. John Wesley, by Charles Wesley, Presbyter of the Church of England*. It was throughout an appeal for loyalty to the Established Church, commencing:

> My first and last, unalienable friend,
> A brother's thoughts with due regard attend. . . .
> Far from the factious, undiscerning crowd,
> Distressed I fly to thee, and *think aloud*;
> I tell thee, wise and faithful as thou art,
> The fears and sorrows of a burdened heart,
> The workings of (a blind or heavenly) zeal,
> And all my *fondness for the Church* I tell,
> The Church whose cause I serve, whose faith approve,
> Whose altars reverence, and whose name I love. . . .

A few phrases must undoubtedly have made John Wesley feel uncomfortable:

> When first sent forth to minister the word,
> Say, did we preach ourselves, or Christ the Lord?
> Was it our aim disciples to collect,
> To raise a party, or to found a sect? . . .

Its full effect on his brother is difficult to gauge, though in June Charles received some rather testy letters from him, including one hinting that even separation might be necessary when the Bishop of London could excommunicate a preacher for not having a licence—'We have no time to trifle!'

During the following months Charles Wesley enlisted the support of other evangelical clergymen, including the

Rev. Samuel Walker of Truro, John Wesley's confidant, to whom he wrote from Bristol on 7th August 1756:

REVEREND AND DEAR SIR,

My brother is coming hither to a conference with his preachers. Another letter from you might, by the blessing of God, confirm him in his calling. He seems resolved to temporize with them no longer. Mr. Grimshaw is coming to strengthen his hands. We shall have a private conference before the general one.

I should have broken off from the Methodists and my brother in 1752 but for the agreement. I think every preacher should sign that agreement or leave us. What I desire of my brother is:—1. That the unsound, unrecoverable preachers should be let depart just now. 2. That the wavering should be confirmed if possible, and established in their calling. 3. That the sound ones should be received into the strictest union and confidence, and as soon as may be prepared for Orders.

To this end my brother ought, in my judgment, to declare and avow, in the strongest and most explicit manner, his resolution to live and die in the communion of the Church of England. 1. To take all proper pains to instruct and ground both his preachers and his flock in the same—a treatise is much wanting on this subject, which he might write and spread through all his societies. 2. To wait with me on the archbishop, who has desired to see him, and tell him our whole design. 3. To advise, as far as they think proper, with such of our brethren the clergy as know the truth, and do nothing without their approbation.

In his next letter to Walker he admitted that:

Lay-preaching, it must be allowed, is a partial separation; and may, but *need* not, end in a total one. The probability of it has made me tremble for years past, and kept me from leaving the Methodists. I stay not so much to do good as to prevent evil. I stand in the way of my brother's violent counsellors, the object both of their fear and hate. . . . The restless pains of bad men to thrust me out from the Methodists seems a plain argument for my continuing with them.

Charles managed to gain a few more signatures to his document binding preachers to the Church, though they were still only a tiny fraction of the whole number. Then came the Conference of 1756, whose 'happy issue' he reported to Walker in the words of his brother's manuscript account (which seems to have disappeared, though it is partly quoted in John Wesley's *Journal*):

'... We afterwards spoke largely of keeping united to the Church; and there was no dissenting voice, but all were knit together in one mind and one judgment.

The subject was resumed on the second and third days; and my brother and I ended the conference with a strong declaration of our resolution to live and die in the communion of the Church of England. We all unanimously agreed, that whilst it is lawful or possible to continue in it, it is unlawful for us to leave it.'

The letter continued:

Meantime I think we have cause to be thankful that hitherto the Lord hath helped us. Satan I trust has done his worst. ... My brother seems farther from a separation than ever. ... He has also undertaken to write a treatise to confirm the Methodists in the Church. Next Monday I expect to set out for the north *on the same errand.*

Writing one of his periodical reports of this northern journey to his brother, Charles added in shorthand:

What passed between you and me about ordaining, if you have forgot, I will never remind you of. . . . Neither shall I dispute with you which is the greatest friend of the Church. You gave me great pleasure by insisting, I am of the two the most likely to leave it. Most glad am I to believe you: and if you stand by it, it is no great matter whether I leave it or no.

Although Charles Wesley was conscious that his own zealous efforts had warded off danger for the time being, he knew that diligence was still necessary. On 23rd October 1756 he wrote to his brother, again in shorthand:

Mr. Walker's letter deserves to be thoroughly considered. Your answer I assent to. One only thing occurs to me now which might prevent in great measure the mischiefs that will probably ensue after your death, and that is, greater, much greater deliberation and care in admitting preachers. Consider seriously if we have not been too easy, too hasty in this matter. Let us pray God to show us if this has not been the principal cause why so many of our preachers have so lamentably miscarried. Ought any new preacher to be received before we know that he is grounded, not only in the doctrine we teach, but in discipline also, and particularly in the communion of the Church of England? . . .

I have but one thing more to offer at present. Is it not your duty to stop Joseph Cownley and (such like?) from railing or laughing at the Church? The short remains of my life are devoted to this very thing, to follow your sons (as Charles Perronet once told me we should follow you) with buckets of water, and quench the flame of strife and division which they have, or may kindle.

The same message he was proclaiming both in his preaching and in his pastoral letters to the societies, such as that to the Leeds Methodists:

I knew beforehand that the Sanballats and Tobiahs would be grieved when they heard there was a man come to seek the welfare of the Church of England. . . . But let not their slanders move you. Continue in the old ship. Jesus hath a favour for our Church, and is wonderfully visiting and reviving His work in her.

Victory seemed near. In November 1757 Charles wrote to Howell Harris:

Our *friend* has agreed with me *to call in his licenses*: I mean, to stop the preachers from qualifying themselves for Dissenting Teachers. I believe *the only way* to keep them steady is the prayer of faith. Our Lord has strengthened my hand by a full persuasion that all things shall work together for good for the furtherance of His Gospel.

In 1759 he was turning his attention from rebel Methodists to sympathetic clergy, telling his wife of a sacramental service held at Lady Huntingdon's, and adding, 'The converted clergy will be multiplied by the time my brother and I finish'.

Then, quite suddenly, the storm broke. In February 1760 three trusted preachers at Norwich, John Murlin,

Paul Greenwood, and Thomas Mitchell, were persuaded to administer the Sacrament of the Lord's Supper. John Wesley heard of it just before he left London for Ireland, but did not seem unduly disturbed, merely asking Charles to go and see what was happening. When they met at Spitalfields Chapel on the evening of 2nd March Charles handed the following letter to his brother, who simply passed it back after glancing through its contents:

DEAR BROTHER,
I have thought and prayed about going to N[orwich], and am ready to go; but not on a fool's errand. Your want of resolution yesterday has saved you reading a long letter. Did you give M[urlin] and his fellows the least check? Did you blame them in the slightest word? What must be the consequences? The rest, secure in your weakness, will do what they list; will sooner than you are aware follow the example of those three, and draw as many disciples after them as they can, into a formal separation.

If your weak conscience will not let you touch them, what signifies my going to Norwich? You will not stand by me: your fear or dissimulation will throw all the blame upon me, or perhaps disown me. Yet for your sake and the people's this I would do. Write a letter by me to the preachers, what you would have them and me to do. Blame them as strongly as your conscience will let you. Otherwise you betray them and all the preachers. You betray your own authority and our children, and our Church, and are the *Author of the Separation*.

I see my first step, which is to secure this people *first*. The Lord, I doubt not, will direct and keep me.

You might answer this from the first place you stop at.

Can you find in your heart to speak word tonight of continuing in the Church of England?

The challenge of the last sentence, so Charles reported to his wife, had some effect, 'for it extorted a few words of exhortation to stay in the Church'. But there was no chance of conversation after the service: 'my best friend was waiting for him, so we shook hands, and parted in silence'. The following day he continued:

My B[rother]'s final resolution (or irresolution) is not to meddle with the Sacred Gentlemen at Norwich *till* the Conference, i.e. *till* they are confirmed in their own evil of pride and practice, and till they have poisoned all the preachers and half the flock.

At the Conference, I presume, he will put it to the vote whether they have a right to administer. Then by a large majority they consent to a separation.

Five months' interval we have to do whatever the Lord directs by way of prevention. If I am to stand in the gap now as formerly, I shall have strength of body given me, and strength of grace. If I cannot act in the spirit of love and meekness, I will go aside into a corner for my few remaining days. . . .

The Fast-day must keep me in town till the 17th. Whether I shall then be sent to Norwich, or elsewhere, I see not yet. But I expect a busy time of it—and no thanks for my pains.

Five months' interval! He started using it speedily. A strong letter was sent off to his brother:

Upon the whole I am fully persuaded *almost all* our preachers are corrupted already: more and more will give the Sacrament and set up for themselves, even before we die: and all except the few that get Orders will turn Dissenters before or after our death.

You must wink very hard not to see all this. You have connived at it too, too long. But I now call upon you in the name of God to consider with me, What is to be done? First, to prevent a separation. 2. To save the few uncorrupted preachers. 3. To make the best of those that are corrupted.

To several of the preachers themselves went pleading letters. To John Johnson:

It has been said that our preachers may baptize and administer the Lord's Supper *without separating from the Church of England*. But are not these two inseparable? A man may shut his own eyes, and fancy no one else can see. But by so deceiving myself, can I deceive others? If my brother and I connive any longer, not only a separation, but general confusion must shortly ensue, and the work of God be destroyed. . . .

'They shall prosper, who love her.' If you love *Her*, you are nearer and dearer to me than all my natural relations. I look upon you as more than my brother, friend, or son. I acknowledge myself your willing servant, your affectionate father, your eternal debtor. All I can do for you as to soul, body, and estate, I ought, I will do, the Lord being *my* helper; and neither life nor death shall separate you from

Your invariable friend
CW

Or again, to Nicholas Gilbert:

I shall tell you my mind plainly, because I love you. My soul abhors the thought of separating from the Church of England. You, and all the preachers know, if my brother should ever leave it, *I should leave him*—or rather *he me*. While ye have any grace remaining, ye can never desire to part *us*, whom God hath joined. You would rather waive your right if you had it (which I absolutely deny) of ordaining yourselves priests, than occasion so great evil. . . . I never professed a friendship and proved false to my profession. I never (that I know) forgot a kindness done me. Your fidelity to the Church of England, although your duty, I shall accept as the greatest kindness you can possibly shew me; beyond any personal benefit whatsoever.

His wife was a little puzzled about the excitement that filled his letters to her, and he had to explain:

We have allowed our lay preachers to take out licences as *Dissenting Protestants*. To the Government they therefore say 'We are Dissenting Ministers'; to the Methodists they say 'We are not Dissenters, but true members of the Church of England.' To a press-warrant or persecuting justice they say again 'We are Dissenters'. To me at our next Conference they will unsay it again. This is their sincerity, and my brother applauds their skilfulness—and his own.

In this interpretation he was certainly unfair, betrayed by his sincere but almost fanatical zeal for the Church. In similar terms he wrote to valiant John Nelson:

I think you are no weathercock. What think *you* then of licensing yourself as a *Protestant Dissenter*, and baptizing and administering the Lord's Supper—and all the while calling yourself a Church of England-man? Is this honest? consistent? just? Yet this is the practice of several of our sons in the Gospel, even of some whom I most loved, and most depended upon. . . . John, I love thee from my heart: yet rather than see thee a Dissenting Minister, I wish to see thee smiling in thy coffin.

In writing to Christopher Hopper he not only re-emphasized his constant claim that it was quite possible for the suitable preachers to become clergy, but answered some of Hopper's grievances about superannuation, showing how they supported his own position in this matter of separation:

MY DEAR BROTHER,
You justly observe, it is not my way to hear one side only; neither (you might add) to answer your reasons by stopping your mouth.
You talk reason in your last, reason which cannot be answered. At least I flatter myself so, because you speak my very heart.
You have not been suffered to speak: your complaints have been slighted: your reasons not attended to: your old worn-out brethren left—to the parish.
'What must be your end?' This question ought to be asked—considered—urged—insisted on—till it be answered to your full satisfaction.
Here is a poor Methodist preacher, who has given up his business (his little all) for the sake of preaching the Gospel. Perhaps he has got a wife, and children, and nothing to keep them. By labouring like an horse, and travelling like a postboy, for ten or a dozen years, his strength is exhausted. Yet he is able, and quite willing, to do what he can still. But how shall he get bread for his family? That Mr. Super-intendent will look to.
Well, be it so. Suppose, neither he nor his children are *starved* while my brother and I live, what must he do when we depart? Our end cannot now be far off. What will then become of this old faithful preacher? 'He must turn Dissenting or Church Minister.' I grant it. There is no medium.
'But will you' (you ask us) 'now use all your interest to get him ordained?' I answer for myself, Yes: and will begin tomorrow, or never blame him for turning Dissenter. Neither have I the least doubt but *the porter will be commanded to open*

the door, and to admit by imposition of hands as many as have addicted themselves to God's service in the Established Church. I have more reason for believing this than is commonly known, and am assured, if our preachers do not ruin themselves and the work by their precipitation, our Lord will take care of every one of them. If any of you prefer the service of the Dissenters, I would let you depart in peace. If your heart is as my heart, and you dare venture in the same bottom, then am I your faithful servant for the residue of my days.

To the Rev. William Grimshaw also went a lengthy letter, accompanied by a copy of John Wesley's *Reasons against a Separation from the Church of England*, which Charles Wesley had reprinted for the occasion. In his reply Grimshaw said:

I little thought that your brother approved or connived at these things, especially at the preachers' doings at Norwich. If it be so: To your tents, O Israel!—It's time for me to shift for myself.—To disown all connection with the Methodists. . . . I hereby therefore assure you that I disclaim all further and future connection with the Methodists.

The public reading of Grimshaw's letter at London 'put them in a flame'. Charles Wesley vividly described the scene to his wife:

All cried out against the licensed preachers: many demanded they should be silenced immediately; many, that they should give up their licences; some protested against ever hearing them more. . . . The lay preachers pleaded my brother's authority. I took occasion from thence to moderate the others, . . . and desired the leaders to have patience till we had had our Conference, promising them to let them know all that should pass at it. They could trust me, I added, that I would not betray the cause of the Church, or deceive them; that I was resolved no one of them all should be deceived or ensnared into a meeting-house. If they chose to turn Dissenters, they should do it with their eyes open. My chief concern upon earth, I said, was the prosperity of the Church of England; my next, that of the Methodists; my third, that of the preachers; that if their interests should ever come in competition, I would give up the preachers for the good of the whole body of the Church of England: that nothing could ever force me to leave the Methodists but their leaving the Church. In that case they would suffer me to be cast off, an old faithful servant, worn out by serving them. You cannot conceive what a spirit rose in all that heard me. They all cried out that they would answer for ninety-nine out of a hundred in London that they would live and die in the Church. My business was to pacify and keep them within bounds. I appointed another meeting this day fortnight, and Friday sennight as a fast for the Church.

Charles had registered another victory. For the time being he had his way. Brother John yielded to entreaty. The offenders at Norwich seem to have been gently rebuked. William Grimshaw did not leave the Methodists, after all. And the following Conference was one of 'love and unanimity'.

CHAPTER IX

PATERFAMILIAS

CHARLES WESLEY was gradually ceasing to itinerate, most of his ministry becoming confined to the south, especially to the neighbourhoods of Bristol and London. The reasons were various. Mainly it was due to his health, undermined by his Georgia privations, and in a parlous condition for years. Pleurisy, neuralgia, lumbago, dysentery, piles, rheumatism, gout, scurvy—a host of ailments make their appearance in his letters, some of them frequently. Soon after the Norwich Sacrament disputes it seemed that his health was breaking up altogether. That same agitation made him realize more clearly the widening gulf between himself and many of the preachers. He shrank from controversy with them, and felt that his time could most profitably be spent in safeguarding the loyal churchmanship of the societies most amenable to his influence—those at Bristol and London. (It is noteworthy that after his death these continued to be strongholds of the 'Church-Methodists'.) Thoughts of itinerating in Ireland he had long ago dismissed for health reasons, and his last extended tour in the north, taking in Birmingham, Nottingham, Sheffield, Leeds, York, Bradford, Bolton, and Manchester, had been undertaken in 1756. His correspondence reveals a longing to make another such tour, a longing frustrated, however, by his feeble health. Even as late as 1773 he was writing 'I do not want a heart to visit my very dear friends at Newcastle, but a body'.

Although health was the main factor limiting Charles Wesley's itinerancy, undoubtedly another contributory reason was his family. At the outset of his married life he had gone out of his way to plead that it would make no difference, and his letters provide clear evidence that he conscientiously tried to follow out this principle. Almost to the end of his days his duties as Methodist preacher and pastor took him away from home for weeks and months at a time—though he certainly grew restive under these absences. For some years he tried to make marriage literally a pilgrimage. After a miscarriage in the spring of 1751 Sally travelled with him on his round of the societies, and accompanied him on preaching tours in later years. In 1752 he wrote to her from Cornwall: 'The *next* time you hinder me in my work will be the first time.' This was in October, shortly after the birth of their son, baptized John Wesley—a sign, especially in those days of rare double names, of Charles's admiration for his elder brother. Of his firstborn son, as is the way with fathers, Charles was immensely proud, though rather shy, defending himself against his wife's hint about his lack of exuberance by answering playfully:

Why, I love him as well again as you do. Only you make the most of a little love, by showing it, and I make the least of a great deal, by hiding it.

Young Jackie only saw one birthday. The winter of 1753–4 brought a double tragedy to the household. With John Wesley at death's door, and busy composing his own epitaph, Charles accompanied him to London, only to hear that his own wife was ill with confluent smallpox. For a month she lay 'struggling in the toils of death', and henceforth her lovely features were so marred by the disease that the nineteen years difference between them was no longer noticeable. Little Jackie caught the infection and died. Once more they were a childless couple. Whilst Sally convalesced with her parents and at Lady Huntingdon's, Charles continued his itinerancy, and later in the year she joined him. The coming of another child again altered the situation, though Martha Maria, as she was called, born in the summer of 1755, lived only a month. The following year found Charles Wesley visiting the north for what was to be the last time.

When in 1757 John Wesley expected Charles to make a similar expedition, he gently declined. Family considerations were confirming physical disability to suggest this course. Home was becoming more and more desirable, so that in the spring he had written:

MY DEAREST OF DEAR ONES,
Absence only increases love: for you are never absent from my heart. I go on heavily without you: and shrink back from the thought of losing you all the summer.

And once more he was about to become a father, and wanted to give his wife, not only the support of his prayers and of his hymns, but of his presence. He was apparently of real use in these trials, and in 1764 wrote that he and nurse Burgess could manage very well without a doctor. On 11th December 1757, Charles junior was born. On 1st April 1759 came another—a girl, as Mrs. Wesley was sure it would be, so that Charles had written in February: 'Whom would you have for the other sponsor in case your Sally proves a Samuel?' Sally it was, however, and the following year another girl was born, Susanna, who lived only eleven months. In 1762 Mrs. Wesley, taking with her Charlie and Sally, aged four and three, accompanied her husband to London for his work there during the summer, and again in 1763. The birth of another short-lived girl, Selina, in 1764, put a stop to travelling. On 24th February 1766 the long-expected Samuel was born, and in December 1767 John James—a fortnight before the proud father's sixtieth birthday. John James, like the earlier namesake of his uncle John, died whilst still a child, in July 1768. By this time the centre of gravity for Charles Wesley had shifted to London, more especially as young Charlie had already proved himself a musical prodigy, whose talents could best be developed there.

As early as 1760 Charles had pondered the advisability of removing to London, whence he wrote to his wife:

As I shall probably take much more public care upon me than I have ever done herebefore, my office will require me to spend more time in town, *perhaps to settle here.*

In 1768 he was examining prospective houses in London, announcing: 'my brother himself is quite pleased with our having an house near London.' Eventually the widow of Colonel Gumley saw them settled down in No. 1 Chesterfield Street, Marylebone, then a pleasant country suburb, rather too distant from the centre of things—the Foundery—for John Wesley's liking. In the spring of 1771 Charles made the final arrangements for the family's removal from Bristol:

Mrs. Ashlin thinks the person now employed in airing the beds &c would be a very proper servant. She is cleanly, sober, diligent, an hearer of the word—though not in society. We shall keep her to keep up the fires, to keep the windows open, and to lie in the beds. When you come you will do—as you like. . . .

Morse [the carrier] will take good care of the harpsichord; but who of the cat? If you cannot leave him in safe hands, Prudence must bring him up in a cage: and if I finish my course here, I may bequeath him to Miss Darby.

Henceforth the family headquarters was at London, though the Bristol house was kept on for some years, and only in 1782 was the furniture remaining there sold up.

Charles Wesley's enforced absences from his wife and children were punctuated, as might be expected, with constant inquiries after their health and progress. Charlie's teething troubles in 1758 caused the anxious father to write:

H

Shall I bring you a necklace for Charly's teeth? Poor lamb! What shall we do to help him? Give for me as many kisses as you please. His many London friends salute him at this distance; being ready, when he is within their reach, to eat him up.

A year later Charlie had the measles—'meazles' as Charles Wesley spelt it—and his wife was naturally anxious about Sally, only two months old. He answered her thus:

My dearest Sally's letter did not reach me till this morning. I was in hopes the worst was over with Charles. The whooping cough does not always accompany the measles; and will not, I trust, in his case. The girl may not have them at all. However, expect them; and expect both the children to be brought safe out of them.

Always there loomed the grim shadow of that dread disease which had ruined Mrs. Wesley's beauty and snatched away their firstborn. In January 1760 he wrote:

My dear Sally's letter this moment received has awakened all my love and concern for our dearest boy. But I hope you will have the comfort while reading this to see him as well as you wish her [sic]. If not, and the Lord is pleased to try us further, let us remember, we are not our own; neither are our children. The most likely way to keep them is to give them up in the spirit of daily sacrifice. I know not what God will do with them; only I know He will do what is best, whether that be to take them early or late to Paradise.

Every illness he has will be in your apprehension the smallpox. I don't think he will have it till he has all his teeth. If your uneasiness for him continues, you must pity, and wean his sister.

Mrs. Wesley had reason to be afraid, however. In 1768 John James died from the foul disease, and it was feared that young Samuel had been infected. Charles wrote home:

Our preparation could not save the first Jacky, because God had prepared a better thing for him. The means may keep

Samuel with us. Let us be thankful that he still holds up. If he should have the distemper soon, I believe it will only lessen his beauty. I long to see him and you, but fear I must be detained another week in town.

Actually Samuel escaped for the time being, though a few years later he did contract smallpox, as did his sister Sally also.

Not only his children's health, but their education and spiritual progress were Charles Wesley's concern. In educational matters he was a disciple of John Locke—and of his own mother. When their first child, John Wesley, was only a year old, he had written to his wife:

The most important of all Locke's rules you will not forget: it is that in which the whole *secret* of education consists—make it your invariable rule to *cross his will*, in some one instance at least, every day of your life. The Lord give you wisdom and resolution to do so. Ask, and you shall find His grace sufficient for you.

This doctrinaire treatment was modified in the case of his second son:

Charley you *need* not chastise too severely, if he is *indeed* so easy to be managed: but I a little doubt a son of mine. You will find by and by he has a will of his own. Persuade him, and you need never compel him. If he will lead, 'tis pity he should drive.

Charles Wesley had strong views on public schools, and did not even send his sons to Kingswood School, preferring to leave their education to Mrs. Wesley and himself, together with the aid of occasional tutors. In 1766 he wrote to his wife:

It is superfluous, yet I cannot help cautioning you about Charles (and Sally too), to take care he contracts no acquaintance with other boys. Children are corrupters of each other.

The postscript to a letter a few weeks later reveals in a parenthesis the strict, formal school in which the Wesley children were reared—they were aged eight and seven at the time:

Do you want anything besides handerchers? Tea I shall scarce forget, or Sally's present. My tenderest love to her and her brother. (By the way, 'tis time they should learn to call each other brother and sister.)

Popular children's books were not banned, however, and his letters home contained references to *Aesop's Fables*, *Robinson Crusoe*, *Gulliver's Travels*, and *Don Quixote*.

The obvious musical talent of his sons prevented Charles from carrying to its logical extreme his principle about crossing their wills. To Mrs. Laroche, a devout lady who objected to eleven-year-old Charlie's playing in concerts he replied:

I always designed my son for a clergyman. Nature has marked him for a musician: which appeared from his earliest infancy. My friends advised me not to cross his inclination. Indeed I could not if I would. There is no way of hindering his being a musician but cutting off his fingers. As he is particularly fond of church music, I suppose if he lives he will be an organist.

An anonymous Quaker who raised objections on the same occasion he thus answered:

My friend's mistake is owing to prejudice of education. I can with a good conscience breed up my son a musician, not to please the giddy multitude, but to earn his bread. Some trades which the Quakers exercise without scruples I think full as dangerous, or more so, than music.

A little tartness crept into his reply:

I do remember Eli; and excuse a Quaker for seeing no difference between encouraging my son in music, or encouraging him in rapine and adultery. . . . I could always throughout my ministry bring up a musical son for a musician. . . . So if sin lieth at the door, then let it lie. God being my helper, I shall not open the door to let it in!

Soon it was clear that his other son would also need to be bred up a musician. Charles Wesley's anxiety that his children should realize that to be Christians was far more important than to be famous musicians is revealed in the following letter to Samuel, aged seven:

London, March 6, 1773.

Come now, my good friend Samuel, and let us reason together. God made you for Himself, that is to be for ever happy with Him. Ought you not therefore to serve and love Him? But you can do neither unless He gives you the power. Ask, (He says Himself) and it shall be given you. That is, pray Him to make you love Him: and pray for it every morning and night in your own words, as well as in those which have been taught you. You have been used to say your prayers in the sight of others. Henceforth, go into a corner by yourself, where no eye but God's may see you. There pray to your heavenly Father who seeth in secret: and be sure He hears every word you speak, and sees everything you do, at all hours and in all places.

You should now begin to live by reason and religion. There should be sense even in your play and diversions. Therefore I have furnished you with maps and books and harpsichord. Every day get something by heart: whatever your mother recommends. Every day read one or more chapters in the Bible. I suppose your mother will take you now, in the place of your brother, to be her chaplain, to read the psalms and lessons when your sister does not. . . .

Foolish people are too apt to praise you. If they see anything good in you they should praise God, not you, for it. As for music, it is neither good nor bad in itself. You have a natural inclination to it: but God gave you that: therefore God only should be thanked and praised for it. Your brother has the same love of music much more than you, yet he is not proud or vain of it. Neither, I trust, will you be. You will send me a long letter of answer, and always look upon me both as

Your loving father and your friend
C. Wesley.

The same spirit is shown in a letter of 1776, in which Wesley announced to James Hutton, with whom his early friendship had been renewed, the lionizing which greeted his sons:

> Mr. M[adan?] intends to carry them both on Wednesday to Mr. Southwell, where Judge Barrington is to bring Bach and a troop of connoisseurs. Charles *will* not play, if he can help it. I am better pleased with his temper on these occasions than if he was the best musician in the world.

Not that Charles Wesley was unresponsive to his sons' triumphs, of course. We can sense his pride in the subdued excitement of a letter to his wife describing the thirteen-year-old Charles's reception in London in February 1771, with its references to musical figures well-known in their day:

> MY MOST DEAR SALLY,
>
> On Saturday, you may remember, we dined with our Islington friends. Mr. Battishill[1] and his agreeable wife were of the party. He began by playing and singing several songs, of the Messiah chiefly. He is entirely of Mr. Kelway's[2] mind with respect to the old and new music, and glad that Charles is instructed in the former *only*: but backward to believe he can as yet play Scarlatti! When Charles played K[elway]'s last sonata and one of Scarlatti's he expressed the utmost astonishment: declared, 'He excelled all the Masters': that he traced K[elway] in every note and every motion; that he could not bear to hear any but him and his master play those sonatas, so hard and yet so excellent: that neither K[elway] nor Scarlatti himself could play Scarlatti's lessons better: that he ought immediately to learn thorough-bass and composition. . . .
>
> Tues. Febr. 26. We called on Mr. Beard,[3] whose kindness to Charles is wonderful. He promised to come and see us the first opportunity. From him we went to the rehearsal of the *Cure of Saul*; and were highly feasted at it. . . .

---

[1] Jonathan Battishill, 1738–1801, organist and composer, buried in St. Paul's Cathedral.
[2] Joseph Kelway, died 1782, organist and composer, and Charles's tutor.
[3] John Beard, 1716?–91, great singer, for whom Handel composed the tenor solos in the *Messiah*.

Thurs. 28. From the rehearsal of *Samson* Mr. Arnold[1] carried us home. Mrs. Arnold fell into an immediate intimacy with Charles; and after dinner treated him with several of Arnold's unprinted sonatas, overtures, &c, any of which he offered Charles; and she offered to give him copies. She plays far better than Rush or any private person I ever heard. Yet Charles would not exchange his manner of playing for hers, quite fashionable, rapid—staccato. . . .

'Tis with great difficulty I find time to write even to you; your son engrossing my whole time and care. Blessed be God for *our* uninterrupted prosperity. May you and your moiety of children enjoy the same.

Eventually the encouragement which Charles Wesley felt compelled to give to his sons' musical ventures, such as the series of subscription concerts in their Marylebone home, brought a challenge from his brother John, which he answered by quoting a document he had drawn up on 14th January 1779:

My reasons for letting my sons have a concert at home are:

I. To keep them out of harm's way: the way (I mean) of bad music and bad musicians, who by a free communication with them might corrupt both their taste and their morals.

II. That my sons may have a safe and honourable opportunity of availing themselves of their musical abilities, which have cost me several hundred pounds.

III. That they may enjoy their full right of private judgment, and likewise their independency: both of which must be given up if they swim with the stream and follow the multitude.

IV. To improve their play and their skill in composing: as they must themselves furnish the principal music of every concert. Although they do not call their musical entertainment a concert. It is too great a word. . . .

Quoting this to his brother after the event, Charles added:

I am clear, without a doubt, that my sons' concert is after the will and order of Providence. It has established them as musicians, and in a safe and honourable way. The Bishop

---

[1] Samuel Arnold (later Dr. Arnold) 1740–1802, editor of Handel's works, as well as a prolific composer in his own right.

[of London] has since sent us word that he has never heard any music he liked as well, and promises Charles five scholars next winter. . . .

They may still make their fortunes if I would venture them into the world: but I never wish them rich. You also agree with me in this. Our good old father neglected every opportunity of selling our souls to the devil.

It was in this same spirit that Charles Wesley warned Charles junior not to hope for too much from his contacts with George III, another of his conquests:

Have you heard from Windsor? I am not sanguine in my expectations from that quarter; neither should you be.

I cannot wish you to play any more at Windsor. It will only stir up a nest of hornets, and set them upon contriving mischief. Your interest is to play least in sight.

To Mrs. Wesley he wrote in 1786:

I am not sanguine in my expectations of good from Windsor. If Charles has received no evil by it, it is a miracle, and I am satisfied.

It was Charles Wesley's care for his musical sons that occasioned what appears to have been his last letter, to a music dealer whose faulty book-keeping had led to an apparent error:

Mr. Wright,
If there is the least doubt, Mr. Wesley always takes the safest, that is, his neighbours' side, choosing to pay a bill twice (or twenty times) rather than not at all.

He will be obliged to Mr. Wright for a line of acknowledgement that he is now out of his debts.

Febr. 13, 1788.

In spite of Wesley's preoccupation with his sons, his daughter was not neglected. Young Sally apparently found his reprimands rather irksome—for eating raw fruit when she was five, for tumbling about on the fashionable high-heeled shoes when she was seventeen, and for wanting to go to balls when she was twenty-four, though in these later years he guided her by an ominous silence rather than by a scolding:

My not forbidding you, I thought was the strongest restraint to a generous mind, who knew what was most agreeable to me.

I never, that I remember, forbade your going to a play. Probably you left off going because you knew it so contrary to my mind. And I took it kindly of you.

His genuine anxiety for her welfare is shown in many letters, such as the following written to her in 1777, when she was on holiday at the home of that well-known portrait painter, John Russell (later R.A.), a great friend of the family:

I think you may avail yourself of my small knowledge of books and poetry. I am not yet too old to assist you a little in your reading, and perhaps improve your taste in versifying. You need not dread my severity. I have a laudable partiality for my own children. Witness your brothers; whom I do not love a jot better than you. Only be you as ready to show me your verses, as they their music.

The evenings I have set aside for reading with you and them. We should begin with history. A plan or order of study is absolutely necessary. Without that, the more you read the more you are confused, and never rise [above] a smatterer in learning.

Sally must have squirmed a little, however, under his commendation of other young ladies to her disadvantage:

I have made a convert here [Bristol] of Miss Chapman's boarder, Miss Morgan, who goes to bed at ten, and rises at six. This good beginning has led her into a regular improvement of all her time. She accompanies me in my daily rides; she follows the plan of study which I have given her; she has got a good part of Prior's *Solomon* by heart. I am now teaching her shorthand: as she is as willing to receive help and instruction as I am to give it.

Why am I not as useful to my own daughter? You have a thirst after knowledge, and a capacity for it. Your want of resolution to rise, and to study regularly, has discouraged me.

Carry but these two points, and behold, I am entirely at your service. Whether your brothers go on or stand still, I would go on constantly in assisting you. I would read something with you every day, and do what good I can for the little time I shall be with you.

Your Ode on Peace I have corrected, at least, if not amended. You must begin immediately to be regular, to be diligent, to be tightly. Thomas à Kempis, I think, you would now relish, and Law's *Serious Call*. Your first hour, remember, is always sacred.

Follow Miss Morgan's example. Be as glad of my help as if I was not your father. If I live another year, I can communicate to you sufficient knowledge to go on without me. It might be of great use to you, if I read the *Night Thoughts* to you, and pointed out the passages best worth your getting by heart. You may take your turn of riding with me, (a dress might be procured), and then we should have many a learned conference.

Although he seems to have been a little heavy-handed with his only surviving daughter (we remember that he was fifty-one when she was born), so that she turned with something of relief to her uncle John, there is no doubt of his deep love for young Sally. And it was to her that he turned for comfort during his last autumn at Bristol, in 1787:

Probably I shall depart without taking leave. My eyes fail me for writing and reading. Perhaps they may not be quite darkened, till they are closed.

In his next letter he added, 'Probably you will have the office of Milton's daughter in my last days'. By October 1787 this prophecy had been fulfilled, and one of his last letters to Miss Briggs was written wholly in the hand of his 'secretary, Sally', to which he appended his signature. And it was with his hand in hers that he died on Saturday 29th March 1788.

CHAPTER X

CURE OF SOULS

CHARLES WESLEY's preaching and poetry were important factors in the spread of Methodism, but without John's administrative genius and calm statesmanship the fire might easily have burned itself out in a generation with little to show where it had been except a renewed group of Christian worshippers here and there. Continually the leaders produced by the revival were hiving off, becoming clergymen or ministers effective only in a limited locality. Sometimes this was because of a genuine fear of a break with the Established Church, sometimes because the strain of itinerancy had proved too much for them. Both causes, as we have seen, operated with Charles Wesley himself, the second-in-command of the Methodist societies. On several occasions he had pondered the advisability of accepting a Church living, but no bishop was ever to institute him to 'the cure and government of the souls' of any English parish. He had come to believe that a higher authority had assigned to him the much more difficult task of remaining firmly planted in the widening gap between Methodism and the Church of England. For the last thirty years of his life, however, this in effect meant a cure of souls, though a very extensive one. The full itinerancy, and the detailed organization of the Methodist preachers and societies, gradually slipped from his grasp, until he became a kind of Anglican missioner, stationed alternatively in two huge parishes, Bristol and London—and finally almost exclusively in London.

His fiftieth year found him mentally and physically exhausted, quite unfitted for the strains under which his amazing brother seemed to flourish, so that Charles could exclaim: 'He is an astonishing youth, and may be saluted, like the eastern monarchs, "O king, live for ever!" ' In June 1758, for instance, Charles wrote to his wife:

> I dined at Miss Chambers's with Mr. and Mrs. Hunt, Mr. and Mrs. Bowls, Mr. Downing, &c. We sang, and prayed, and talked on the one thing, not without life and comfort. Yet was I thoroughly tired before we parted. I cannot away with more than three or at most four in company. A crowd ever of religious people dissipates me, unless we spend the whole time in worship. I believe I shall quite come over to you, and never stir from home except to visit the sick or to preach.... My love of retirement increases with my business, and I should not be sorry if all the religious world cast me off.

Even his preaching, indeed, had to be curtailed, and in February 1759 he wrote home:

> I am as careful of myself as you can wish me—and a good deal too careful in the judgement of some. My brother had set me down for preaching every night in the week, at every quarter of the town. I regard not *his* commands of this (sort?), and plainly told him so.

Charles pined for the life of a country clergyman, something like the studious retirement of the Epworth rectory. When returning from Georgia in 1736 he had voiced these feelings to his brother John:

> *Pray ask Mr. [Oglethorpe?], who knows me better than I do myself, these two questions;*
> *1. Whether he thinks me fit to be trusted with the care of souls?*
> *2. Whether I could have a small village remote from any town, where I may hide myself from all business and all company?*

The same desire for a quiet, localized ministry was expressed to his wife from London a month after their marriage:

> I took sweet counsel with our select brethren how to make the most of a short life. In mine, I want more action and

more retirement, and acquainted them with my resolution to appropriate all my mornings to study or self-improvement, and all my afternoons to visiting from house to house. We applied to our Lord for strength to fulfil the desires he gave us; and I am persuaded, as to myself, that my latter end will be better than my beginning.

That he was eminently successful as a pastor in Bristol and London is evidenced by the people's love for him, the sacrifices that they were ready to make on his behalf, and their willingness to join forces with him even against his more ambitious and far-seeing brother. His letters abound with examples showing how he handled the spiritual problems of the souls under his care. Here, for instance, is his rather drastic method of dealing with the self-satisfied backsliders who were all too frequent in the early days of the revival, as outlined in a letter of October 1740 to his brother:

A soul that answers *your* description I would deal with in *your* manner. But suppose a justified person settled again upon his lees, and by his *past* graces strengthening himself in his *present* wickedness (whether of heart or life). I would not tell such an one he never was justified, but that he was now in a far worse state than if he never had tasted the grace of God from which he is fallen. That he NEVER CAN recover till he comes to Christ as he did at first, a poor damned unjustified sinner—*stripped of all*. But while he rests in his former comforts he is worse than a publican, worse than even a *gross* Pharisee, inasmuch as he is now a subtle, inward, spiritual Pharisee and trusts in the abuse of mercy. Out of this [strong]hold I would drive and thrust him down into the deep of his sin and misery. Neither, till he humbles himself under the mighty hand of God, can he ever be exalted or restored.

He went on to quote concrete examples, as well as further to discuss the spiritual principles upon which his pastoral work was based:

E.g. Ann Holton (once justified) is now in the false assurance of faith; lives in all worldlymindedness, passion and reviling:

but for all that she says no man shall rob her of her confidence. She *will not*, no she *will not* receive the sentence of death in herself, and must therefore sink with her broken reeds into Hell.

N. Bath is not *so* proud as she *was*.

Mrs. Labbe[1] too, stops short on this side Jordan, and no one shall persuade her her heart is not changed *in part*. . . .

B. Sayse is one of a better spirit, yet him also would I bring into the deep of humility. He began to be lifted up, thought something of himself, despised and told his wife he was *more spiritual* than her. My weapons were mighty through God to the pulling down of his strongholds, yet would I not tell him that I now think him humble, (or rather, less proud), for *my* heart showeth me the wickedness of his, that was I to observe it to him, he would be proud of his humility. . . .

I cannot but think we agree in the general that everyone who is settled, but not on Christ, should be unsettled again. When God *has* given faith, I am firmly persuaded, He gives *some measure* of true humility *before* He gives me a rooted love; that is, *before* I am in Christ a new creature I shall feel myself in Adam a fallen spirit.

Over twenty years later he was urging even more strongly the dangers of spiritual pride, writing to Joseph Cownley:

You believe a man perfect because he says 'I am': that's the very reason for which I believe, and am sure, he is not perfect.

Letters written under the influence of deep emotion enable us to watch him by the death-beds of his people, as that of young Alexander White in 1748:

Today after giving him the Sacrament I asked how he was. He told me Satan had been buffeting him two nights ago, 'and made me think my heart was divided between God and the world. And I offered God my heart, and He would not take it for a while. But I cried to Him so much the more that He might take it. And He did at last: and He will keep it to all eternity.'

I asked if he was easy now? 'Yes: the Wicked One touches me not. I am kept in perfect peace.' Whether his pain did not trouble him? 'No. The Lord bears all my burdens.'

[1] The name is written in shorthand.

'Then pain is little to you?'

'It is nothing: the comfort is so much greater that it quite swallows it up.'

'Do you think we shall know one another in Paradise?'

'I can make no doubt of it. I go a few moments before to tell our elder brethren you are coming after.'

I asked him to pray for me. 'That', said he, 'I cannot help, while I am in the body; and I now pray my God to bless you and make you a burning and a shining light—which you are.' He then kissed my hand with great eagerness. I kissed him, and in mighty prayer we commended his spirit to God. About a dozen of us were witnesses and sharers of his triumph.

Many of the people who came under the influence of the Methodists were making their first contact with personal religion, and their newfound experience was given its seal in baptism or re-baptism—often by immersion. A note written by Charles Wesley in 1739 to the Bishop of Bristol, Dr. Joseph Butler, is of interest:

MY LORD,

Several persons, both Quakers and Baptists, have applied to me for baptism. Their names are W. Crease, Mary Crease, Mary Gregory, Rebecca Dickenson, Anne Apanin, Eliz. Mills, Eliz. Parsons. It has pleased God to make me instrumental in their conviction. This has given them such a prejudice for me that they desire to be received into the Church by my ministry. They choose likewise to be baptized by immersion, and have engaged me to give your Lordship notice, as the Church requires.

The experience of a London Methodist baptized by him is described in a letter of 1758:

Yesterday I saw Mrs. Bird. At her baptism [a few days earlier] she was quite overpowered, and struck speechless. Now she tells me, in going home that night such joy sprung up in her heart as she never felt before: a joy unspeakable and full of heaven. It lasted all night. She could have rejoiced to give up her spirit then, knowing she should be saved eternally. Since then she has been frightened at the withdrawing, or at least abatement, of her happiness. I told her she must expect temptation as well as comfort, and our Lord's own baptism was immediately followed by temptation.

Sometimes the circumstances were even more unusual, as in 1774 at Bristol:

I have had with me this month or more two very extraordinary scholars and catechumens: two African princes, carried off from Old Calabar by a Bristol captain after they had seen him and his crew massacre their brother and three hundred of their countrymen. They have been six years in slavery, made their escape hither, were thrown into irons, but rescued by Lord Mansfield, and are to be sent honourably back to their brother, king of Calabar. This morning I baptized them. They received both the outward visible sign and the inward spiritual grace in a wonderful manner and measure.

Occasionally his pastoral duties even involved exorcism:

Fri. Aug. 15 [1766]. Breakfasted again with Mrs. H[ervey?]. The last time, she informed me of the house being disturbed by an invisible lady (as was supposed) who died there last summer in despair. Mrs. H. herself was kept several nights from sleeping by the noises. I prayed that she might not be disturbed by any beings visible or invisible; and she has never heard it since, although the rest of the family constantly do.

Not only do Charles Wesley's letters *reveal* his methods and success as a pastor; they themselves *were* a method, and a very valuable one, by which he exercised his cure of souls. In 1751, for instance, when he felt himself near to death, he wrote to his brother from Leeds:

I laboured to hold up as long as I could, but was forced at last to follow their advice and lie down. Expecting to grow worse, I disburdened my soul by writing to a dear friend who was grown slack and weary of the narrow way. I warned and besought him with many tears to repent and do the first works. Then the fever came, and being put to bed, I lay burning and restless (but not comfortless) all night.

Sometimes he sent pastoral letters to particular societies, in the manner (and with much of the phraseology) of St. Paul himself:

To my beloved brethren at Leeds, &c.
Grace and peace be multiplied! I thank my God on your behalf for the grace which is given unto you, by which ye stand fast in one mind and in one spirit. My Master, I am persuaded, sent me unto you at this time to confirm your souls in the present truth, in your calling, in the old paths of Gospel-ordinance. O that ye may be a pattern to the flock for your unanimity and love! O that ye may continue stedfast in the Word, and in fellowship, and in breaking of bread, and in prayer, (private, family, and public) till we all meet around the great white throne!

Letters of consolation naturally loomed large in his correspondence. He wrote to Joseph Cownley on the loss of his wife:

London, June 9, 1774.
MY DEAR BROTHER,
It is the Lord! Let Him do as seemeth Him good. He has taken away the desire of your eyes with a stroke; but He does not forbid you to feel your loss, like Ezekiel. It is a great thing that you can submit, and *patiently* bear your irreparable loss. By and by you will *feel* the comfort of *calm* and perfect resignation. Perhaps you may not be *joyful* in tribulation till through much tribulation you are entered the kingdom.
You shall go to her, and *then know* perfectly the love of your Father in this severe affliction, and comprehend *how all* the paths of the Lord are mercy and truth.

He would not allow sorrow to be overdone, however. A year after the death of grand old Vincent Perronet, 'Archbishop of the Methodists', he wrote thus to Perronet's grand-daughter, Miss Elizabeth Briggs:

'*Sad* anniversary of his translation,' do you call it? And your 'loss irreparable?' The day was the most joyful and happy he ever knew; and your loss is momentary, and reparable in a happy eternity. We ought only to rejoice and give thanks for his having been lent to the world near a century. Therefore from this time, observe, I can allow you to mourn no more.

Spiritual exhortation was continually on his lips and in his letters. His brother Samuel's widow did not escape. Shortly before her death he wrote:

By nature we are averse to the things of God. We are *born* unbelievers; and have no faith till we are *born again*. This is a hard saying (and yet a kind one) that you, my dear sister, *are not yet born again*. O let me beseech you to ask our dear Lord whether these things be so. If you have not experienced this change, there stands an *impossibility* betwixt you and salvation. For 'except a man be born of the Spirit he cannot enter into the kingdom of heaven: and without holiness no one shall see the Lord.' Do not (I again conjure you) slight my words, for you *now want something without which it is impossible for you to be saved*. If you will consent to see your want, Jesus Christ will *supply* it. For it is no other than Himself, even 'Christ in *you* the hope of glory.'

To the end of his life he was thus commending personal religion to apparently unsympathetic readers. In 1776, after visiting young Charles's tutor Joseph Kelway, he wrote a letter that caused him much mental exercise, as is shown by the draft, with its many erasures:

Nov. 23, 1776.
DEAR SIR,
The joy I felt at seeing you on Monday somewhat resembled the joy we shall feel when we meet again without our bodies. Most heartily do I thank God that He has given you a longer continuance among us; and, I trust, a resolution to improve your few last precious moments. *We* must confess at *our* time of life that 'one thing is needful', even to *get ready for our unchangeable eternal state*. . . . You are convinced of my sincere love for your soul, and therefore allow me the liberty of a friend. As such I write, not to teach you what you do not know, but to stir up your mind by way of remembrance, and exhort both you and myself

> Of little life the most to make
> And manage wisely your last stake.

After this favourite quotation from Abraham Cowley he went on to describe in detail the nature of true repentance, such as he felt that Kelway even yet needed, signing himself 'the faithful servant and friend of your soul, CW'.

The family of the Rev. Vincent Perronet of Shoreham had a particularly warm place in his affections. A number of letters survive which were written to Perronet's son William, a young army surgeon:

Manchester, Oct. 23, 1756.
DEAR WILL,
'Watch and pray.' Watching implies early rising. 'Pray:' that is, enter into thy closet. The first hour should always be sacred. Carry this point, and the world, the flesh, and the devil, shall fall before you.

'A few minutes for prayer' are far better than none at all: but prayer never hinders business. 'Wholly taken up' therewith, yet begin the day in the spirit of prayer and sacrifice: so shall you thrive indeed, and whatsoever you do it shall prosper.

Your faithful friend,
Charles Wesley.

Bristol, March 25, 1758.
DEAR WILL,
... Your last but one mentions 'business and variety of company as a remedy for your dejection of spirits.' Strange that one who has tasted the true medicine of life should talk so idly! If you have forsaken the fountain, in vain do you hew out broken cisterns. They can hold no water. Despair of help till you recover your first love. Acquaint yourself again with Christ, and be at peace. I pray God deliver you from every show and shadow of happiness, and *keep you miserable*, till you see and find happiness in Him.

Charles Wesley's score of letters to Ebenezer Blackwell, ranging over the years 1746 to 1753, are full of exhortations most appropriate to a man of money:

O my dear friend, work for God, before the night cometh. Labour for the meat that endureth to life eternal. With all thy gettings, get wisdom. Make friends of the mammon of unrighteousness. Lay up treasure in heaven. Let the Master when He cometh find you watching.

Bristol, May 13, 1752.

DEAR SIR,

I have often had it on my mind to tell you my *friendly fears*, lest your engagement with the gentlemen of your Club should insensibly draw you in further than you were aware into the ways and spirit of the world. Perhaps by sly you might be led even into their diversions, which you know can never be done to the glory of God. Perhaps you may by little and little become partaker of their sins, at least by your *silence* at their idle words or *paths*. There's no standing neuter in the midst of worldly men.

Another great business friend of the Wesleys, Samuel Lloyd, was similarly challenged when his commercial activities continued far longer than seemed good:

MY DEAR SIR,

. . . I have neither right nor desire to know the state of your affairs. Neither have I ever had one careful thought about you. The blessing of God is with you; that is enough. I trust Him for my friends as well as for myself. All my trouble is that there seems no end of your toils on this side eternity. A few calm days *should* conclude so various a life.

Four years later he was still writing in similar vein:

Bristol, Febr. 27, 1768.

MY DEAR SIR,

It seems as if we had forgot each other. We shall shortly meet in the land where all things (temporal or grievous) are forgotten; therefore let us lose no time to secure the one thing needful. Our only business now is

> Of little life the most to make,
> And manage wisely our last stake. . . .

Tell me, if you can, that you are less hurried in business, better in health, calmer in mind, poorer in spirit, and you will give great satisfaction to, dear sir,
Your faithful loving servant,
C. Wesley.

Friendly exhortation could be transformed into searing rebuke when occasion demanded. Such seemed to be the case with Richard Moss, former Methodist preacher, who had successfully concealed his bigamy from the Wesley brothers for many years, and had deceived Charles Wesley into 'marrying' him:

What can I say to one who was my friend, whom I loved so well, and trusted so entirely? . . . [I] give you up for a ——. I cannot write the word. I cannot express my thoughts, or the horror of my soul at what you have done—what you have been! My brother's thoughts are as mine. Every honest and good man's judgment is the same. You know our mind in Mrs. B.'s. How can you bear to think on that worthy injured woman? On your having made me the instrument of her ruin? On your having abused my brother by such an heap of lies, such a train of deep dissimulation? On your having given such a wound to religion, and brought such a reproach on a whole innocent people?

This is not the language of passion. I write without railing or aggravations.

You married your first and *only* wife 28 years ago.[1] You came soon after to us, and abused our credulity with a false story. Me you told that you had been drawn in while a thoughtless boy, and forced to marry a common whore in a fit of drunkenness; that you left her when sober and never saw her more. You told my brother her name was Moll Platt. We believed you. You turned a strict Methodist, was received by my brother with the utmost confidence. Married another woman; had several children by her. Professed perfection, while living for years in known wilful adultery. Buried her: made use of me to deceive another, a gentlewoman of family and fortune: robbed her of the last: paid some of your debts with her money; left her behind to pay the rest. Gathered all together, and went missioner to America.

Now you must have been all this time either an hypocrite or a self-deceiver. If an hypocrite, the deepest I ever heard or read of. In all your prayers, singings, tastings, communicatings, exhortings, preachings, was you or could you be carrying on the cheat? If so, you cannot believe the word of

[1] 26th December 1741, as shown by the certificate which Charles Wesley quoted in full.

the Bible. You cannot believe there is either heaven or hell, or God or devil. But you was only a self-deceiver? This can hardly be conceived. Your smooth soft way might and did blind others; but could you thereby blind yourself? Was you not conscious of what you had done? If you did persuade yourself that all was right, then you was given up by the just judgement of God to strong delusion to believe it: your heart was hardened and your conscience sealed. And if there is a God who judgeth the earth, He is your Enemy, and if there is an hell it is your portion.

As Charles Wesley claimed, this is not impassioned writing; but it bites deep. These are the words of a man to whom human souls mattered greatly, to whom the fair name of religion was very precious. Although he had gone into what seemed comparative retirement by the side of his brother's tireless wanderings, he was still desperately concerned about his task as one of the shepherds of Christ's flock, a task which had been outlined in weighty words by the Bishop of London at his ordination into the priesthood:

to be messengers, watchmen, and stewards of the Lord; to teach, and to premonish, to feed and provide for the Lord's family; to seek for Christ's sheep that are dispersed abroad, and for His children who are in the midst of this naughty world, that they may be saved through Christ for ever.

CHAPTER XI

ORDINATION IS SEPARATION

WE have seen how the year 1760 marked a climax in Charles Wesley's efforts to keep the Methodists sailing in 'the old ship' of the Church of England. For another quarter of a century he continued a losing warfare against the forces which made for separation. He was glad to support a few of the younger preachers in their desire to enter Holy Orders, writing to disappointed Joseph Benson (a future President of the Conference) in 1772:

> It is the Lord who wills you to preach with *His* commission *only*. You ought not to have repented of having offered yourself for the outward call. Whenever *it is best* you shall have *that* also. . . . I cannot help believing that you *will be* called to the sacerdotal as well as the prophetic office. Let not my good friends Cownley and Hopper infect you with *their* prejudices. Give not place to the least disaffection to the Church of England. God has a favour to her; more, I am persuaded, than to any national Church in Christendom.

He also played an active part in securing new clerical blood for Methodism, answering the Rev. Mark Davis's objections thus:

> 'You understand it is matter concluded on that the people are to be directed by twelve lay preachers.' You misunderstand their misinformation. All which we would or can do for keeping them together after our departure is to commend them to the most solid and stablished of our preachers (be they twelve, or more, or less) whom we advise to keep close together, and regulate the society as near as may be according to their old rules. Now this is impossible without a clergyman or two at their head. Wherefore my brother has so often and so warmly invited you to come and help them, before we leave them. . . . I suppose your informer made you believe you must be under the government of lay preachers, whereas

in the very nature of things both they and the society *must* be under your government.

The preachers themselves, of course, were not too happy about this, especially in the case of Davis, who was fickle and rather untrustworthy, and also expected what they considered too high a salary. Their opposition Charles summed up thus, in May 1773:

The salary is a mere pretence. The true and only objection is your Orders. T[homas] O[livers], A[lexander] M[ather] &c will not be so much wanted, so much respected, so well paid, and so important (they foresee) if any clergyman succeed to the care of this flock. . . . But the bridle is in their jaws. The Founder and Head of the Church of England is against them, and I firmly believe the bulk of the poor Methodists will never turn Dissenters, but continue in the Ship till we are all brought safe to the haven.

To ensure this an understanding had already been reached that John Wesley's successor in supreme charge of the Methodist societies should be the saintly vicar of Madeley, Charles's old friend John Fletcher, though his health proved to be even more feeble than that of Charles himself.

Not only did Charles Wesley strive to hold Methodism securely within the Established Church, but also to bring the English Moravians back to the fold by means of union with the Methodists. During the preliminary negotiations with James Hutton in 1771, however, he made quite clear his loyalty to Methodism:

DEAR JAMES,
Take it for granted that I am *fixed, resolved, determined, sworn* to stand by the M[ethodists] and my B[rother] right or wrong, through thick and thin. . . . Notwithstanding my incurable bigotry, can you and will you love me? If so I am your man, your first and latest of friends, your
faithful old CW

By the end of the year he had managed to bring his brother John and Hutton together, and two years later the friendly negotiations were still in progress. Charles's letter of Christmas Day, 1773, contains his favourite Talmudic phrase, which is perpetuated at the head of his memorial in the City Road Chapel, and also on the Wesley tablet in Westminster Abbey:

God will look to that matter of successors. He buries His workers, and still carries on His work. Let Him send by whom He will send. Rather than they should degenerate into a dead formal sect, I pray God the very name of Moravian and Methodist may die together! But I believe with Amos Comenius, that God has a special regard to the Church of England, . . . and that our Lord will have a true Church, a living people in this island, till He comes to set up His Universal Kingdom.

James Hutton proved rather touchy, however, and the conversations eventually came to nothing, though as late as July 1786 Charles was writing to another prominent Moravian, the Rev. Benjamin Latrobe, about the threatened separation from the Church of England:

The friendly intercourse of your Society and ours might be another likely means of preserving our children in their calling. My brother is very well inclined to such a correspondence. . . . If our Lord is pleased to use us as peacemakers under Him, we may yet do something towards preventing any separation at all. . . . The great evil which I have dreaded for near fifty years is a schism. If I live to see that prevented, and also to see the two sticks, the Moravian and English Church, become one in our Saviour's hand, I shall then say, 'Lord, now lettest Thou Thy servant depart in peace'.

The possible union with the Moravians was a side-issue, however. The attempt to keep Methodism within the Anglican Church was Charles's life-work. The opening of the cathedral of Methodism, the 'New Chapel', in City Road, London, in 1778, provided a rallying-point for his supporters. The fact that it was under the supervision of Anglican clergy, however, was a challenge to the travelling preachers, and there was friction between them and Charles, who wrote to John:

> I have served the chapel morning and evening, and met the society every other week since you left us. I think myself bound so to do as long as I can; both by my duty as a clergyman, and by our agreement when the chapel was first opened. . . . Many of our subscribers, you know, were not of our society, but of the Church: out of good-will to them and to the Church, not out of ill-will to the preachers, I wished the Church service continued there.
>
> I am sorry you yielded to the preachers. They do not love the Church of England. What must be the consequence when we are gone? A separation is inevitable.

John Wesley himself had occasion to test his own supreme power over the Methodist preachers, by removing from the superintendency at Bristol a preacher, Alexander McNab, who refused to recognize an Irish clergyman stationed by Wesley at Bath, which was then in the Bristol circuit. A fierce though short-lived controversy ensued, during which Charles reported to his brother:

> [McNab] bitterly complained of your taking too much upon you: of your interfering with the Assistant, appointing him one week and displacing him the next, &c. He [said] 'The *Ministers* [i.e. the preachers] were resolved to have a meeting shortly, and to settle among themselves the affairs of the Church.' So it will not be a Congress, but a Synod—if they can *agree* to choose a Moderator. Mr. Carlisle assures me they are determined to make a separation, for their patience can hold out no longer. One would think they took the Americans for their pattern.
>
> By the time that their Synod is opened, I hope your *sound* sons will be ready to meet you in a lawful assembly. God has suffered them thus to show themselves before your death that you may save a remnant, divide the prey with the mighty, and bequeath your children to faithful pastors.

On December 6th 1779 Charles added further details, including McNab's words, 'I think it my duty to pray for the death of Mr. J. W.':

Supposing you as good as dead, they begin to divide the spoils. Bristol and Bath are Mr. McNab's and Bristol's share. The latter expected to reign a second year in this place; and surely you could not be so provokingly vivacious as to hold out beyond that time. Having the power in their own hands, they never suspect you *to rebel*, or to act with such vigour against them. In your second infancy they held your leading strings, and out of pure compassion they intended at the next Conference to spare your age the burden, and take upon themselves *the care of all the Churches*. . . .

Lose not this precious, this last opportunity, of establishing your authority for the rest of your days. You, single, are no match for near two hundred smooth-tongued men. Rouse yourself, before they flay you alive for your skin. Begin proving your sons one by one. Pray for wisdom, resolution, and love. I would give up my wife and children, to cleave to you, if you stand firm and faithful to yourself, and the cause of God, and the Church of England.

On this occasion John Wesley did vindicate his authority, though he reinstated the rebel, which Charles thought a sign of weakness.

Another shadow was looming large. At this very time some of the preachers were clamouring for ordination, not by a bishop, but at the hands of John Wesley himself. When Charles heard of it, and was asked by his brother to attend the 1780 Conference, where the matter would probably be discussed, he replied:

My reasons against accepting your invitation to the Conference are:
1. I can do no good.
2. I can prevent no evil.
3. I am afraid of being a partaker of other men's sins, or of countenancing them by my presence.
4. I am afraid of myself; you know I cannot command my temper, and you have not courage to stand by me.
5. I cannot trust *your resolution*: unless you act with a *vigour* that is not in you, *conclamatum est*.

I am not sure they will not prevail upon you to ordain them. You claim the *power*, and only say, 'It is not probable you shall ever exercise it.' Probability on one side implies probability on the other, and I want better security. So I am to stand by and see the ruin of our cause! You know how far you may depend on me: let me know how far I may depend on you and on our preachers.

Actually he did attend, though he kept in the background, as 'some sort of check to the independents'. It was not until four years later that his brother took the long-threatened step of exercising that power of ordaining which Charles denied he ever had. The immediate cause was the need of America, grievously short of ordained clergy.

The desperate plight of America is well known. John Wesley believed that it called for desperate remedies—though he knew that his brother could never agree. So Charles was not informed. On 1st and 2nd September 1784, in semi-secrecy, John Wesley ordained three preachers to serve the American Methodists. The number included Dr. Thomas Coke, already a clergyman, whom Wesley ordained as 'superintendent'—a term naturally enough interpreted as 'bishop', for it conferred his own authority for ordaining American preachers.

It was not until two months later that Henry Durbin, one of Charles Wesley's Bristol correspondents, broke the news to him:

I have heard a report of a curious nature, which believe is well founded and was done when you were in Bristol, though perhaps unknown to you, that Mr. Creighton was sent for from London to join in an ordination of presbyters, and that at five in the morning, supposed at Mr. Castleman's the two preachers were ordained, and after Dr. Coke was ordained presbyter (so they undoctored him) by your brother and Mr. Creighton according to a new form, and with power to ordain others in America.

Charles replied:

Your last is this moment arrived. I am thunderstruck. I can[not?] believe it.

Soon he was reading his brother's printed vindication, dated 10th September. Blinded by his own ingrained prejudice in favour of episcopal ordination, however, he still could not follow the logic of John Wesley's position, and was inclined to set it all down to the machinations of Dr. Coke. He wrote to Durbin:

The apology has so stunned and con[fuse]d me that I have not yet recovered the use of my brain. . . . He is the dupe of his own cunning. He thought he could do what he would with the Doctor; and the Doctor has done what he would with him. . . . [He said] 'that he would never separate from the Church without my consent.' Set this then to his age: his memory fails him. . . .

I have the satisfaction of having stood in the gap so long, and staved off the evil for near half a century. And I trust I shall be able, like you, to leave behind me the name of an honest man. Which with all his sophistry he can never do. . . . I call you . . . to witness that I have had no hand in this infamous ordination.

Constantly he was excusing his brother's conduct by references to his great age—he was eighty-one. To John himself, however, he wrote somewhat tartly:

What foul slanderers those (enthusiasts?) are! How have they for three score years said (John Wesley was?) . . . a Papist: and lo he turns out at last a Presbyterian!

He shared his sorrows and fears with Rev. Vincent Perronet at Shoreham, and also with an American clergyman, Dr. Thomas Bradbury Chandler, for whom he wrote an account of Methodism which Chandler apparently used to good effect in reclaiming American Methodists for the Anglican Church. Extracts from this letter, written on 28th April 1785, have already been quoted. Longer excerpts must now be given, for it is one of the most important documents which Charles Wesley penned, a kind of *Apologia pro Vita Sua*. Of the Georgia mission he wrote:

Our only design was to do all the good in our power, as ministers of the Church of England, to which we were firmly attached both by education and principle. (My brother still acknowledges her the best national Church in the world.)

The ecclesiastical dangers of the widespread preaching which they had both undertaken after their experiences of May 1738, said Charles, had been recognized and guarded against:

Still we had no plan but to serve God and the Church of England. The lost sheep of that fold were our principal care, not excluding any Christians of whatever denomination who were willing to add the power of godliness to their own particular form.

Our eldest brother Samuel was alarmed at our going on [*sic*], and strongly expressed his fears of its ending in a separation from the Church. All our enemies prophesied the same. This confirmed us the more in our resolution to continue in our calling; which we constantly avowed both in public and private, by word and preaching and writing, exhorting all our hearers to follow our example.

My brother drew up rules for our Society, one of which was 'Constantly to attend the Church prayers and Sacrament. . . .'

When we were no longer permitted to preach in the churches, we preached (but never in church hours) in houses or fields, and sent (or rather carried) from thence multitudes to church who had never been there before. Our Society in most places made the bulk of the congregation both at prayers and Sacrament.

I never lost my dread of a separation, or ceased to guard our societies against it. I frequently told them 'I am your servant as long as you remain members of the Church of England; but no longer. Should you ever forsake her, you would renounce me'.

After outlining the beginnings of Methodism, Charles went on to his interpretation of the crucial stage through which they were then passing:

Some of the lay preachers very early discovered an inclination to separate, which induced my brother to publish his *Reasons against a Separation*. As often as it appeared we beat down the schismatical spirit. If anyone did leave the Church, at the same time he left our Society. For near fifty years we kept the sheep in the fold; and having fulfilled the number of our days, only waited to depart in peace.

After our having continued friends for above seventy years, and fellow-labourers for above fifty, can anything but death part us? I can scarcely yet believe it, that in his eighty-second year my brother, my old intimate friend and companion, should have assumed the *episcopal character*, ordained elders, consecrated a bishop, and sent him to ordain the lay preachers in America! I was then in Bristol, at his elbow; yet he never gave me the least hint of his intention. How was he surprised into so rash an action? He certainly persuaded himself that it was right.

Lord Mansfield[1] told me last year that ordination was separation. This my brother does not, and will not see, or that he has renounced the principles and practice of his whole life; that he has acted contrary to all his declarations, protestations, and writings, . . . and left an indelible blot on his name as long as it shall be remembered!

Thus our partnership here is dissolved, but not our friendship. I have taken him for better for worse, till death do us part—or rather re-unite in love inseparable. I have lived on earth a little too long, who have lived to see this evil day.

In spite of these words about the partnership with his brother being dissolved, Charles Wesley continued to preach in Methodist pulpits, and to save as many as possible from the impending separation. In August 1785, for instance, he was at Bristol, fortifying the Methodists there against the separatist tendencies of Dr. Coke:

For above an hour I exhorted the society to repent and do the first works: then, to continue in the ship. When the Doctor comes to turn them all Dissenters, I trust he (and his king) [*sic*] will be completely disappointed.

It was whilst at Bristol that he heard of his brother's further ordinations, this time of three preachers who should minister in Scotland. Sorrowfully he wrote to his wife:

[1] An old school friend of Charles Wesley, and for thirty years Lord Chief Justice of England.

You think right: 'What has been done already has fixed the preachers Dissenters.' Who would not live fourscore years for so glorious an end. To turn seventy thousand Church of England people, Dissenters! My brother cannot undo what he has done. *His* bishop may now ordain all the preachers without his leave: or the three Scotch presbyters may do it (and will) without either of them. Surely I am in a dream! Is it possible that J. W. should be turned Presbyterian? J. W. the schismatic grandson to J. W. the regicide! How would this disturb (if they were capable of being disturbed) my father and brother in Paradise!

He endeavoured to restrain his brother from still further ordaining:

Bristol, August 14, 1785.

DEAR BROTHER,

I have been reading over again your *Reasons against a Separation*, printed in 1758, and your *Works*; and intreat you, in the name of God, and for Christ's sake, to read them again yourself, with previous prayer, and stop, and proceed no farther, till you receive an answer to your inquiry, 'Lord what wouldest *Thou* have me to do?' . . .

Before you have quite broken down the bridge, stop, and consider! If your sons have no regard for you, have some regard for yourself. Go to your grave in peace: at least suffer me to go first, before this ruin is under your hand. . . . I am on the brink of the grave. Do not push me in, or embitter my last moments. Let us not leave an indelible blot on our memory; but let us leave behind us the name and character of honest men.

This letter is a debt to our parents, and to our brother, as well as to you, and to

Your faithful friend.

Their correspondence was inconclusive, however, and on 27th September Charles worked off steam in a letter to Mr. E. Johnson, a Bristol Methodist who reported John Wesley as saying that:

he never intended to ordain but for America and Scotland, and that the preachers were under the strictest promise to use none of their power in England, but entirely to confine it to these two places.

To which Charles replied:

His charity believeth all things, even the preachers' promises 'not to use their powers in England.' Who can keep them faithful to their promises, when he is in his grave? Who will be bound for the rash Doctor? My brother has given the staff out of his own hands. Either the Doctor or the three Scotch elders may ordain all our preachers without my brother's leave. He has set open the flood-gates: but all who are in the ark are safe.

'He wishes to have things continue in the same channel.' That is, to have us shut our eyes till we open them in the Doctor's Meeting-house (his new Methodist Episcopal Church, I should say.)

His design is to leave the whole Society houses, books, papers, &c, in the hands of his heir apparent and successor, the hot hair-brained Superintendent of North America. My design (and I am persuaded, God's) is to leave you in the bosom of your mother, and I continually pray God that *His* counsel may stand.

It is a very large concession of his that I mean well; yet it is true. For I mean to save him against his will, to make his end like his beginning, to preserve the flock from the wolf's keeping—from being scattered, stolen and destroyed.

In 1786 there seemed some hope that John Wesley had come round to his brother's point of view, and Charles decided to struggle along to support him at the Conference, writing to his wife:

My brother is once more become a champion for the Church: and who so great as he and I? But—but—but! When the Conference is over, we shall see farther. It will cost me some of my last and most precious hours.

He soon discovered, however, that his 'Right Reverend brother' was bent on ordaining Dr. Coke's three missionaries, as well as two more preachers for Scotland. The day before the ordinations took place he wrote:

Bristol, July 27, 1786.

DEAR BROTHER,

I cannot rest, living or dying, unless I deal as faithfully with you as I am persuaded you would deal with me if you was in my place and I in yours.

I believe you have been too hasty in ordaining. I believe God left you to yourself in that matter, as He left Hezekiah—to show you the secret pride which was in your heart. I believe Lord Mansfield's decisive words to me, 'Ordination is separation.'

Thus I have discharged my duty to God and His Church, and approved myself your faithful friend and

Affectionate brother,
CW.

Stop here; ordain no more, but follow your own advice to Mr. H.: 'Spread this letter before the Lord, and He will give you light and strength.'

Despite this letter the ordinations took place. Apparently the brake was being slowly applied, however, and on 29th July Charles wrote to his wife:

My dearest partner will be pleased to hear the result of our Conference. The Dissenting party made a bald push for a separation, strongly urging my brother to ordain a preacher for a desolate place in Yorkshire. John Atlay made a noble stand against them, and fairly conquered them all, with the Doctor at their head. Pawson and those of his leaven could have torn him to pieces, believing him all their own and the most zealous Republican. He proved that ordination was separation. My brother thanked him. All agree to let my brother and me remain in the Old Ship, till we get safe to land.

Happily he was not spared to see what he would undoubtedly have considered a still greater breach between Methodism and the Church of England—the ordination at last, in August 1788, of a preacher to serve the English societies. By that time Charles Wesley had been lying in his quiet grave in Marylebone churchyard for just four months.

CHAPTER XII

SWEET SINGER

At the Conference of 1788, John Wesley placed the following record on the minutes, under the question 'Who have died this year?':

Mr. Charles Wesley, who, after spending fourscore years with much sorrow and pain, quietly retired into Abraham's bosom. He had no disease; but, after a gradual decay of some months

'The weary wheels of life stood still at last.'

His least praise was his talent for poetry: although Dr. Watts did not scruple to say, that 'that single poem, *Wrestling Jacob*, was worth all the verses he himself had written'.

Tribute to his courage under persecution, his pioneer labours for Methodism in different parts of the British Isles, his soul-stirring sermons, his fifty years' devotion as a Christian pastor, his humility, his burning sincerity, even in rebuking his brother, his passionate attachment to the Church of England—all are included in that typical understatement, 'his least praise was his talent for poetry'.

His *least* praise! To later generations, naturally enough, Charles Wesley's hymns have been hailed as his greatest contribution to the Methodist revival, and on them securely rests his fame. The 'sweet singer' of Methodism provided in his robust scriptural song both spiritual education and an inspiring means of giving expression to the richly varying experiences of those pressing along the highway of personal religion.

The chief material for a study of Charles Wesley as poet is to be found in the thirteen volumes of the collected

Poetical Works of the two brothers, and perhaps we should not expect his letters to throw much new light on the subject. It should be noted, however, that some of the poems included in volume eight of the *Poetical Works* were never published by him, but were rescued from letters and private papers. A goodly number still remain unpublished, some enshrined in his correspondence. An adequate study of this most important aspect of Charles Wesley's life, however, is not possible from the limited materials available in his letters. This concluding chapter, therefore, can only aim at providing a few sidelights on Charles Wesley's supreme work as the poet of the Methodist Revival.

His own appreciation of poetry is constantly being revealed by his letters. We are not thinking of his love for the Greek and Latin classics, which he frequently quoted to fellow-clergymen and members of his own family, but of his quotations from English poetry, especially that of Spenser, Milton, Prior, and Young—tastes which he held in common with his brother John. Again like John Wesley, he was fond of the writings of their elder brother Samuel, and found it a great joy to visit Samuel's daughter at Barnstaple in 1758, and to look through his brother's manuscript poems, of which he made copies. He was not quite so enthusiastic about some of his father's verse, as is shown by a letter of 1747 from Ireland:

Passed the evening very agreeably at a Baptist's, a woman of piety and understanding, although a great admirer of my father's *Life of Christ*. She doubly honoured me for his sake, and would needs lend me the book. I have given it a reading, and subscribe to the author's own judgment of it—that the verses are (some of them) tolerable, the notes good, but the cuts best of all.

As we have seen, he endeavoured to nurture the poetic gift which lay dormant in his own daughter, though not with any conspicuous success. Young Samuel, also, had some poetic talent, and was hailed by his father as 'my brother poet'.

Charles Wesley's first extant poem, if such it can be called, was an embryo letter in verse to his brother John, which we have quoted. Maturer epistles in this decasyllabic couplet form followed in later years, a batch of them in 1755, one (that to his brother) being published at the time, whilst the others were apparently prepared for publication, though probably intended in the first place as a rather unusual form of private correspondence and admonition. Only one more, that to George Whitefield, was eventually published by Charles himself. The others are not without interest, however. As an example can be taken the opening of the challenge to Howell Harris, former stalwart of Welsh Methodism:

> Awake, old soldier!—to the fight half-won,
> And put thy strength and put thine armour on!
> Nor dream thyself a vessel cast aside,
> Broken by stubborn will, and marred by pride.
> Most proud, self-willed, and wrathful as thou art,
> Yet God hath surely seen thy simple heart,
> Quenched with His blood the oft re-kindled fires,
> Nor ever left thee to thy vain desires,
> But saved ten thousand times from Satan's power,
> And snatched thee from the gulph wide yawning to devour.
> Then let our Saviour God have all the praise,
> And humbly call to mind the former days
> When He, who waked thy soul to second birth,
> Sent forth a new-born child—to shake the earth,
> To tear the prey out of the lion's teeth,
> And spoil the trembling realms of Hell and death,
> By violent faith to seize the kingdom given,
> And open burst the gates of vanquished heaven. . . .

Even in this conventional couplet form there is no doubt of Charles Wesley's metrical skill, and few minor poets of his day could achieve such disciplined strength. When it came to the lyric, of course, he was well in advance of most contemporary poets, though sometimes betrayed by his fluency into monotonous repetition, as well as into an occasional false rhyme, misplaced accent, or clumsy elision. It must be remembered, of course, that although many of his poems were composed in the quiet of his study at Charles Street or Chesterfield Street, others were written as he jog-trotted along on horseback, as when he wrote in 1755, 'I crept on singing or making hymns, till I got unawares to Canterbury'. Sometimes the conditions were far from propitious, as on a journey seeking the advice of Rev. Vincent Perronet about the obstacles hindering his marriage to Sally Gwynne. This was in January 1749, on the 15th of which month he wrote to her:

The following hymn employed me in my dark wet journey to Shoreham:

> Stop, foolish tears! The God of love,
> Who orders all in heaven above,
>   Who orders all beneath,
> His Providence is on my side,
> And through a wretched life shall guide,
>   And through an happy death. . . .

And so on, for seven unpublished verses, including this versification of Philippians 1^{21}:

> To die in Christ is greatest gain,
> To die—is but to lose my pain,
>   To win a doubtful race,
> A weary pilgrimage to end,
> And grasp my Everlasting Friend,
>   And see His loveliest face.

Often these mentally-composed hymns needed some touching up when being prepared for publication, as most of them eventually were. In 1755, for instance, Charles Wesley wrote to his wife, who was expecting a baby:

Take an imperfect hymn just as it came to my mind:

> Lord, I magnify Thy power,
>   Thy love, and faithfulness,
> Kept to my appointed hour
>   In safety and in peace:
> Let Thy providential care
>   Still my sure protection be,
> Till a living child I bear,
>   And give it back to Thee. . . .

When this poem was eventually published in his *Hymns for the Use of Families*—with an additional verse—there were a few slight emendations, including the alteration of the last line of the opening verse to 'A sacrifice to Thee'.

Charles Wesley's letters contain hymns celebrating various special occasions: 'After Preaching the Gospel in Cornwall, 1746'; 'Thanksgiving for our Deliverance from Shipwreck'; and, of course, death-bed scenes like that of Alexander White in 1748:

It bore me all day as on eagles' wings. I felt when the happy soul was going, and under the sense thereof began the following hymn:

> 1. O what a soul-transporting sight
>   Mine eyes to-day have seen,
>   A spectacle of strange delight
>   To angels and to men!
>   Nor human language can express
>   Nor tongue of angels paint
>   The vast mysterious happiness
>   Of a departing saint. . . .

When eventually published this poem extended to fourteen such verses! Sometimes, however, there came from his pen just a few simple lines, as on the death of 'sister Pearson' in 1764:

I asked, 'Are you afraid to die?' 'O no,' she answered, 'I have no fear: death has no sting: Jesus is all in all.'

> How did I ev'n contend to lay
>   My limbs upon that bed!
> I asked the angels to convey
>   My spirit in her stead.

Sometimes the poem included in his letter was a prayer for recovery, like that written for his great friend Rev. John Fletcher in 1776, and sung by the congregation at Bristol—to be copied out and sent by Charles Wesley to Fletcher's wife during another illness shortly preceding his death in 1785. Sometimes it was called forth by controversy such as that at Bristol in 1779, when Alexander McNab had wished for John Wesley's death:

> Jesus, Thy hated servant own,
> And send the glorious Spirit down
>   In answer to our prayers.
> While others curse, and wish him dead,
> Do Thou Thy choicest blessings shed,
>   And crown his hoary hairs.

Affairs of national importance, too, inspired his muse, as they were reflected in many of his letters. The Gordon Riots of 1780, for instance, he described vividly both to his brother and to his daughter Sally, and one of his letters to her contained the draft of a poem which was later published as one of the *Hymns written in the Time of the Tumults*.

Most of the poems contained in Charles Wesley's letters, however, were on various family occasions. The period of his courtship with Sally Gwynne was particularly fruitful of these emotional outpourings, though it must be admitted that, as we have seen, they were quite different from the conventional love-lyrics of the eighteenth century versifier. Sally continued through the years to be one of his chief inspirations. Hurrying home to reach his sick wife in August 1749, he wrote to her:

Part of an hymn I send, without time to finish it:

> 1. See, gracious Lord, with pitying eyes!
>   Low at Thy feet a sufferer lies
>   Thy fatherly chastisement proves,
>   And sick is she whom Jesus loves!

2. Thy angels plant around her bed,
   And let Thy hand support her head,
   Thy power her pain to joy convert,
   Thy love revive her drooping heart!

3. Thy love her soul and body heal,
   And let her every moment feel
   Th' atoning blood by faith applied,
   The balm that drops from Jesus' side.

4. ———

My time is out. Farewell, and a thousand times, Farewell in the Lord, thy peace, thy strength, thy life eternal!

Their setting up house in Bristol was commemorated by his 'first Family Hymn', part of which he sent in a letter to Ebenezer Blackwell, as quoted elsewhere. The approach of their first wedding anniversary also naturally called for a poem, especially as Charles was at the other side of the country at the time:

I have barely time to transcribe an hymn for April 8, if we live so long, and commend you to the tender mercies of God in Christ Jesus!

Hymn for April 8

1. Sweet day, so cool, so calm, so bright!
   The bridal of the earth and sky!
   I see with joy thy cheering light
   And lift my heart to things on high.

2. My grateful heart to Him I lift
   Who did the guardian angel send,
   Enriched me with an heavenly gift,
   And blessed me with a bosom-friend. . . .

5. God of eternal power and grace,
   I bow my soul before Thy throne;
   I only live to sing Thy praise,
   I live and die to Thee alone.

> 6. My more than life to Thee I give,
>   My more than friend to Thee restore,
>   (When summoned with Thyself to live),
>   And fall, and silently adore.
>
> 7. Yet if Thy welcome will consent
>   To spare her yet another year,
>   With joy I take whom Thou hast lent,
>   And clasp her to my bosom here. . . .

All these poetical efforts were not of equal merit, of course, and for various reasons a number of them were not included by him in his published work, or if included were either emended or altered to obscure some particular personal reference. The word 'imperfect' he sometimes added to verses, when he knew either that he had not reached the end of the line of thought which he was following, or that the poem was deficient in poetic merit and needed much 'polishing'. The latter is surely the case with a poem on the first anniversary of the death of his first-born:

> 1. Hail the *sad*[1] memorable day
>   On which my Isaac's soul took wing!
>   With us he *would* no longer stay
>   But soaring where archangels sing,
>   Joined the congratulating quire,
>   And swelled their highest raptures higher.
>
> 2. His soul, attuned to heavenly praise,
>   Its strong celestial bias showed,
>   And fluttering to regain its place,
>   He broke the cage, and reached his God,
>   He pitched in yon bright realms above,
>   Where all is harmony and love &c
>   Imperfect.

These verses reveal how sadly Charles Wesley could sometimes sink, even when trying to express deeply-felt

---

[1] As an alternative, the word 'glad' was added in the margin.

emotion. The reason seems to be that he had forsaken the direct for the involved, the simple for the sophisticated.

We can best take our leave of him by quoting another poem almost worthy to be placed by the side of his own 'Gentle Jesus, meek and mild', though strangely enough he never published it. The verses are contained in a letter written from London on 5th April 1760, which was intended to reach his family at Bristol in time for the eleventh anniversary of his wedding:

Sat. Night.
I dined with Mrs. Galatin alone: prayed, sung with the family; drank tea with my hostess; began an hymn for my dearest friends, as follows:

1. God, be mercifully near,
   Object of my father's fear,
   Me into Thy favour take,
   Me preserve for Jesu's sake.

2. With Thy kind protection blessed,
   Calm I lay me down to rest,
   All I have to Thee resign,
   Lodge them in the Arms Divine.

3. Her, my dearest earthly friend,
   To Thy guardian love commend.
   Day and night her Keeper be,
   Knit her simple heart to Thee.

4. Make the little ones Thy care,
   Bear them, in Thy bosom bear,
   Marked with the Good Shepherd's sign,
   Keep my lambs forever Thine. &c.

I may send the rest in my next. It is time to bid you goodnight. . . . The Lord be your Lord and God forever.

We turn from our study of Charles Wesley as revealed by his letters with a sense that we have been in a spiritual world quite foreign to many Christians of today, a world of the aching sorrows of sin, the throbbing joys of salvation and the utter renunciation of self. To some it may seem not only foreign, but unreal, a fantastic dream-world of the soul, a self-induced hypnotism miscalled faith, and strangely mingled with human errors of judgement. Whether we are attracted or repelled by Charles Wesley's heightened spiritual temperature, however, one thing cannot be questioned—his utter sincerity. There is a depth of feeling both in his letters and his hymns that may be simulated, yet which defies the counterfeiter's art. It is seen in the simplicity of the verses quoted above, and in the closing benediction. He was a man of deep mystical experience, yet deeply sensitive also to the joys and anxieties of common life. Home ties helped to prevent his becoming impersonal, a danger which his brother John did not always avoid. It is undoubtedly because the poet of Methodism thus had both a profound personal faith and a spirit remarkably sensitive to the spiritual needs of others that he was able, not only to supply both outlet, impetus, and education to the religious aspirations of his day, but also to make his unique contribution to the hymnody of the Universal Church.

INDEX

This Index does not purport to be exhaustive. Although references to a few outstanding people and subjects are included, its main function is to list the recipients of the letters quoted. The names of these correspondents are printed in SMALL CAPITALS, and the references are complete to the point of including quotations even where the recipient's name is not mentioned in the text.

America, 88–9, 134–5, 138–9. Cf. Georgia.

BENNET, JOHN, 73–5, 79–80, 86–7. Cf. 71–2.
BENSON, JOSEPH, 88, 129
Bible, use of, 38–9
BLACKWELL, EBENEZER, 39, 44–6, 48–50, 67, 69, 125–6. Cf. 60.
BRADBURN, SAMUEL, 89–90
BRADFORD, JOSEPH, 88–9
BRIGGS, MISS ELIZ., 123–4. Cf. 116.
BUTLER, DR. JOSEPH, Bishop of Bristol, 121
Byrom's Shorthand, 4–6, 26–7, 58

CHANDLER, REV. DR. T. B., 135–7. Cf. 7, 14, 20.
CHAPONE, MRS. SARAH ('Varanese'), 21–4. Cf. 10, 15–16, 28.
Churchmanship, 17, 33–4, 38, 91–103, 117, 129–40
COKE REV. DR. THOMAS, 90, 134, 137–40
Conversion, 23–4, 32–4. Cf. 124.
Courtship, 55–66. Cf. 11–12.
COWNLEY, JOSEPH, 53, 81, 120, 123

Darney, William, 86
DAVIS, REV. MARK, 129–30
Death, 116, 140–1
longing for, 21, 27–8, 33, 45, 66, 68
Depression, 13–14, 20–4, 33, 45, 65–6
DURBIN, HENRY, 134–5

Education, 7–14. Cf. 109–10.
Evangelism, 20–1, 37–8, 49, 73, 124–6

Fenwick, Michael, 83, 85
Fletcher, Rev. John, 130, 146

Georgia, 20–31, 135–6. Cf. America.
GIBSON, DR. EDMUND, Bishop of London, 54. Cf. 20, 128.
GILBERT, NICHOLAS, 100
Grimshaw, Rev. William, 86, 95, 102–3
GWYNNE, MISS SARAH, 43, 45, 50, 53–67, 144. Cf. WESLEY, MRS. SARAH.
GWYNNE, MRS. SARAH, 63. Cf. 60, 64–5.

HARRIS, HOWELL, 97, 143. Cf. 45.
HOLLAND, WILLIAM, 52–3
HOPPER, CHRISTOPHER, 101
Humour, 9, 11, 16, 27, 43, 110
HUNTINGDON, SELINA, COUNTESS OF, 83–5. Cf. 97, 105.
HUTTON, JAMES, 20–1, 28, 31, 111–12, 130–1
Hymns. *See* Poetry.
Hymns and Sacred Poems, 25, 63–4

Illness, 25, 27–31, 42, 56, 68–9, 83, 85, 105, 116–18, 122
Ireland, 44–53, 56–9
Itinerancy, 42–3, 68–9, 79–83, 104–5, 117

JOHNSON, E., 138–9
JOHNSON, JOHN, 99
JONES, MRS. R., 7
Journal, 2, 24, 32, 44, 46–8, 55, 59, 74–6, 81, 92

KELWAY, JOSEPH, 124–5. Cf. 112.
Kirkham, Robert, 9–10, 14–15

LAROCHE, MRS. ELEANOR, 110
LATROBE, REV. BENJAMIN, 131
LEEDS SOCIETY, 97, 123. Cf. 82–5.

LLOYD, SAMUEL, 126
LUNELL, WILLIAM, 50–2

McNab, Alexander, 132–3, 146
Marriage and family life, 66–71, 104–16, 145–9. Cf. 53, 59, 78.
Maxfield, Thomas, 34–5, 40, 82
Methodist Conferences:
  1748, 49
  1751, 86–7
  1755, 93
  1756, 96
  1760, 99, 103
  1780, 133–4
  1786, 139
Methodist preachers, 48, 79–103, 129–33
Money matters, 9, 17–18, 46, 63–4
Moravians, 28, 32, 40–1, 52, 131–2
Morgan, William, 14–15
MOSS, RICHARD, 127–8
MURRAY, GRACE, 72. Cf. 70, and BENNET, JOHN.
Music, 107, 110–14

NELSON, JOHN, 81, 100–1

Oglethorpe, General James, 20, 24–6, 28, 31, 54, 118
OGLETHORPE, MRS. J., 25
Oxford University, 8–18, 28

Pastoral duties, 24–5, 117–28
Perronet, Charles, 46–7, 92, 97
Perronet, Edward, 62, 76–7
Perronet, Rev. Vincent, 48, 60, 123–5
PERRONET, WILLIAM, 122, 125
Persecution, 25, 30, 34–5, 44–6
Poetry, 9, 25, 32, 52, 58–9, 61, 65–7, 71, 94, 141–50. Cf. 86.
Prayer, 38, 57, 67, 77, 111, 125
Preaching, 32–42, 47, 50, 118
Publishing, 63–4, 70, 94, 102

QUAKER, A. 110

RANKIN, THOMAS, 89
Retirement, love of, 22–3, 27, 40–1, 46, 71, 118, 144

Sacraments:
  Baptism, 121–2
  Lord's Supper, 14–15, 17, 42, 47, 92–3, 97–101, 136
SELLON, REV. WALTER, 92–3
SHENT, WILLIAM, 86–7

'Varanese.' See CHAPONE, MRS.

WALKER, REV. SAMUEL, 95–6
Webb, Capt. Thomas, 88
WESLEY, CHARLES, jun. (1757–1834), 78, 114. Cf. 107–13.
WESLEY, REV. JOHN (1703–91), 8–16, 24, 26–8, 30, 34–42, 46–8, 68, 82–3, 85, 88, 91, 94, 96, 98, 113, 118–20, 132–5, 138–40, 142
  Ordinations by, 92–3, 96, 133–40
Wesley, Mrs. John, 75–8
WESLEY, REV. SAMUEL (1662–1735), 17. Cf. 19, 142.
WESLEY, REV. SAMUEL (1691–1739), 17–19, 31. Cf. 7–8, 25, 28, 136, 142.
WESLEY, SAMUEL (1766–1837), 111. Cf. 106, 109, 142–3
WESLEY, MRS. SARAH (1726–1822), 33, 37, 42, 69, 77–8, 93–4, 97, 99–100, 102–3, 105–10, 112–14, 118–22, 137–40, 144–9, Cf. GWYNNE, MISS SARAH.
WESLEY, MISS SARAH (1759–1828), 115–16. Cf. 106, 108.
Wesley, Mrs. Susanna, 13, 19, 29–30, 109
WESLEY, MRS. URSULA ('Nutty'), 18, 124. Cf. 8, 12.
Wheatley, James, 81, 83
WHITEFIELD, REV. GEORGE, 30, 33–4. Cf. 29, 34–5, 41–2, 71, 73, 88, 143.
Williams, Thomas, 48–9
WRIGHT, H., 114
Wright, Hetty (Wesley), 8

ZINZENDORF, COUNT, 29

www.ingramcontent.com/pod-product-compliance
Lightning Source LLC
Chambersburg PA
CBHW071505150426
43191CB00009B/1418